Albert Camus

THE GUEST

The schoolmaster was watching the two men climb toward him. One was on horseback, the other on foot. They had not yet tackled the abrupt rise leading to the schoolhouse built on the hillside. They were toiling onward, making slow progress in the snow, among the stones, on the vast expanse of the high, deserted plateau. From time to time the horse stumbled. Without hearing anything yet, he could see the breath issuing from the horse's nostrils. One of the men, at least, knew the region. They were following the trail although it had disappeared days ago under a layer of dirty white snow. The schoolmaster calculated that it would take them half an hour to get onto the hill. It was cold; he went back into the school to get a sweater.

He crossed the empty, frigid classroom. On the blackboard the four rivers of France, drawn with four different colored chalks, had been flowing toward their estuaries for the past three days. Snow had suddenly fallen in mid-October after eight months of drought without the transition of rain, and the twenty pupils, more or less, who lived in the villages scattered over the plateau had stopped coming. With fair weather they would return. Daru now heated only the single room that was his lodging, adjoining the classroom and giving also onto the plateau to the east. Like the class windows, his window looked to the south too. On that side the school was a few kilometers from the point where the plateau began to slope toward the south. In clear weather could be seen the purple mass of the mountain range where the gap opened onto the desert.

Somewhat warmed, Daru returned to the window from which

Translated by Justin O'Brien. Reprinted from *Exile and the Kingdom* by Albert Camus, translated by Justin O'Brien. © Copyright 1957, 1958 by Alfred A. Knopf, Inc., by permission.

her or meeting her at home. I left it to her to telephone me and wait for me in the café, not every evening, but now and then. Carlotta came every time, devouring me with her eyes. Her voice trembled as we parted.

"I've never seen him since," she whispered one evening.

"You're doing the wrong thing," I replied. "You ought to try and get him back."

It irritated me that she regretted leaving her husband, as beyond all doubt she did. It also annoyed me that she had hoped to bind me closer to her by talking like that. Such futile love was not worth Carlotta's remorse or my own risk.

One evening I phoned her to say I would drop in and see her. She seemed incredulous and uneasy as she opened the door to me. I looked around apprehensively. She was wearing her velvet dress. I remember she had a cold and kept pulling at her handkerchief, dabbing her red nose.

I saw at once that she understood. She was quiet and docile, responding to all I said with timid glances. She let me go on talking, watching me furtively over her handkerchief. Then she stood up, came over to me and leaned against my face; I had to kiss her.

"Aren't you coming to bed?" she whispered in her usual voice.

I went to bed, and all the time I found her face objectionable, damp and inflamed as it was from her cold. At midnight I jumped out of bed and started dressing. Carlotta switched on the light and looked at me a moment. Then she put it out and said to me: "All right then, go." Puzzled and embarrassed, I stumbled out.

For days after that, I feared a telephone call, but nothing disturbed me. Week after week I worked in peace. Then one evening I was seized with desire for Carlotta, but shame helped me to withstand it. Yet I knew that if I had knocked on her door, I should have brought happiness. That certainty I have always had.

I did not yield, but a day or two later I passed in front of her café. There was a blonde at the cash-desk. She must have changed her hours. But I didn't see her in the evening, either. I thought she might be ill, or that her husband had taken her back. That idea displeased me.

But my legs shook under me when the concierge at the street door stared at me with her hard eyes and told me bluntly that a month ago they had found her dead in bed, with the gas turned on.

(*1st—3rd January*, 1938)

CONTINENTAL
SHORT STORIES
The Modern Tradition

CONTINENTAL SHORT STORIES

The Modern Tradition

Edited by

EDWARD MITCHELL

&

RAINER SCHULTE

OHIO UNIVERSITY

W · W · NORTON & COMPANY

New York · London

W. W. Norton & Company, Inc., 500 Fifth Avenue, New York, N.Y. 10110
W. W. Norton & Company Ltd., 37 Great Russell Street, London WC1B 3NU

Library of Congress Catalog Card No. 68-12186
PRINTED IN THE UNITED STATES OF AMERICA
4567890

ISBN 0-393-09797-8

Contents

Preface

Even a cursory survey of presently available short story texts reveals that the vast majority are heavily weighted in favor of English and American tales; and those anthologies which do contain European material tend to emphasize the authors, and the most often read stories, of the nineteenth century. Although we are fully cognizant of the debt which modern literature owes the masters of the late nineteenth century, and while we admire the unquestionable excellence of modern English and American short fiction, it seemed that an anthology devoted exclusively to continental, and chiefly contemporary, authors would fill a distinct need.

Two general criteria governed the choice of selections. First, and foremost, was the desire to include those authors and works which, in our opinion, most adequately represented the present and immediate past masters of continental short fiction. Clearly, and for obvious reasons, that intention is here only partially realized. Second was the intention of presenting the reader with selections which, significant and representative, were not tiresomely familiar. This in part accounts for the fact that the stories by Benn and Böll appear here for the first time in translation.

Convinced that instructors and students alike prefer to engage fiction directly and cope with it in their own terms, we have reduced editorial apparatus to a minimum. Also resisted was the temptation to classify stories by type, or by theme, or as illustrations of plot and character and so forth. Obviously, many of the selections here can be profitably compared and contrasted; and taken collectively, they represent a wide range of practices in employment of point of view, development of character, and rendition of narrative. We have suggested some of the possibilities for comparison and illustration in the study guide questions which are available upon request. However, because structuring is the prerogative of the instructor, we have attempted to leave him free to use this collection in the manner best calculated to meet his needs. For this reason, even the order of appearance in the text represents only the most general progression of stories from the more traditionally existential variety to more contemporary attitudes and concerns.

An anthology which spans even fifty years, particularly if those years are in the twentieth century, will necessarily reflect considerable variety. Our afterword describes a basic framework — one codified enough to be useful, yet flexible enough to accommodate variations—within which these stories can profitably be viewed. Still, the enjoyment and usefulness of any collection of short stories resides ultimately in the stories themselves. Both first and last, it is to the stories that the reader will find himself directed.

CONTINENTAL
SHORT STORIES
The Modern Tradition

Jean-Paul Sartre

THE WALL

They pushed us into a big white room and I began to blink because the light hurt my eyes. Then I saw a table and four men
behind the table, civilians, looking over the papers. They had
bunched another group of prisoners in the back and we had to
cross the whole room to join them. There were several I knew and
some others who must have been foreigners. The two in front of
me were blond with round skulls; they looked alike. I suppose they
were French. The smaller one kept hitching up his pants; nerves.

It lasted about three hours; I was dizzy and my head was empty;
but the room was well heated and I found that pleasant enough:
for the past 24 hours we hadn't stopped shivering. The guards
brought the prisoners up to the table, one after the other. The four
men asked each one his name and occupation. Most of the time
they didn't go any further—or they would simply ask a question
here and there: "Did you have anything to do with the sabotage of
munitions?" Or "Where were you the morning of the 9th and what
were you doing?" They didn't listen to the answers or at least
didn't seem to. They were quiet for a moment and then looking
straight in front of them began to write. They asked Tom if it were
true he was in the International Brigade; Tom couldn't tell them
otherwise because of the papers they found in his coat. They didn't
ask Juan anything but they wrote for a long time after he told
them his name.

"My brother José is the anarchist," Juan said, "you know he isn't
here any more. I don't belong to any party, I never had anything
to do with politics."

Translated by Lloyd Alexander. From *Intimacy* by Jean-Paul Sartre.
Copyright © 1948 by New Directions. Reprinted by permission of the
publisher, New Directions Publishing Corporation. Published in England
by Neville Spearman Limited.

They didn't answer. Juan went on, "I haven't done anything. I don't want to pay for somebody else."

His lips trembled. A guard shut him up and took him away. It was my turn.

"Your name is Pablo Ibbieta?"

"Yes."

The man looked at the papers and asked me, "Where's Ramon Gris?"

"I don't know."

"You hid him in your house from the 6th to the 19th."

"No."

They wrote for a minute and then the guards took me out. In the corridor Tom and Juan were waiting between two guards. We started walking. Tom asked one of the guards, "So?"

"So what?" the guard said.

"Was that the cross-examination or the sentence?"

"Sentence," the guard said.

"What are they going to do with us?"

The guard answered dryly, "Sentence will be read in your cell."

As a matter of fact, our cell was one of the hospital cellars. It was terrifically cold there because of the drafts. We shivered all night and it wasn't much better during the day. I had spent the previous five days in a cell in a monastery, a sort of hole in the wall that must have dated from the middle ages: since there were a lot of prisoners and not much room, they locked us up anywhere. I didn't miss my cell; I hadn't suffered too much from the cold but I was alone; after a long time it gets irritating. In the cellar I had company. Juan hardly ever spoke: he was afraid and he was too young to have anything to say. But Tom was a good talker and he knew Spanish well.

There was a bench in the cellar and four mats. When they took us back we sat and waited in silence. After a long moment, Tom said, "We're screwed."

"I think so too," I said, "but I don't think they'll do anything to the kid."

"They don't have a thing against him," said Tom. "He's the brother of a militiaman and that's all."

I looked at Juan: he didn't seem to hear. Tom went on, "You know what they do in Saragossa? They lay the men down on the road and run over them with trucks. A Moroccan deserter told us that. They said it was to save ammunition."

"It doesn't save gas," I said.

I was annoyed at Tom: he shouldn't have said that.

"Then there's officers walking along the road," he went on, "supervising it all. They stick their hands in their pockets and smoke cigarettes. You think they finish off the guys? Hell no. They let them scream. Sometimes for an hour. The Moroccan said he damned near puked the first time."

"I don't believe they'll do that here," I said. "Unless they're really short on ammunition."

Day was coming in through four airholes and a round opening they had made in the ceiling on the left, and you could see the sky through it. Through this hole, usually closed by a trap, they unloaded coal into the cellar. Just below the hole there was a big pile of coal dust; it had been used to heat the hospital but since the beginning of the war the patients were evacuated and the coal stayed there, unused; sometimes it even got rained on because they had forgotten to close the trap.

Tom began to shiver. "Good Jesus Christ I'm cold," he said. "Here it goes again."

He got up and began to do exercises. At each movement his shirt opened on his chest, white and hairy. He lay on his back, raised his legs in the air and bicycled. I saw his great rump trembling. Tom was husky but he had too much fat. I thought how rifle bullets or the sharp points of bayonets would soon be sunk into this mass of tender flesh as in a lump of butter. It wouldn't have made me feel like that if he'd been thin.

I wasn't exactly cold, but I couldn't feel my arms and shoulders any more. Sometimes I had the impression I was missing something and began to look around for my coat and then suddenly remembered they hadn't given me a coat. It was rather uncomfortable. They took our clothes and gave them to their soldiers, leaving us only our shirts—and those canvas pants that hospital patients wear in the middle of summer. After a while Tom got up and sat next to me, breathing heavily.

"Warmer?"

"Good Christ, no. But I'm out of wind."

Around eight o'clock in the evening a major came in with two *falangistas*. He had a sheet of paper in his hand. He asked the guard, "What are the names of those three?"

"Steinbock, Ibbieta and Mirbal," the guard said.

The major put on his eyeglasses and scanned the list: "Steinbock . . . Steinbock . . . Oh yes . . . You are sentenced to death. You will be shot tomorrow morning." He went on looking. "The other two as well."

"That's not possible," Juan said. "Not me."

The major looked at him amazed. "What's your name?"

"Juan Mirbal," he said.

"Well, your name is there," said the major. "You're sentenced."

"I didn't do anything," Juan said.

The major shrugged his shoulders and turned to Tom and me. "You're Basque?"

"Nobody is Basque."

He looked annoyed. "They told me there were three Basques. I'm not going to waste my time running after them. Then naturally you don't want a priest?"

We didn't even answer.

He said, "A Belgian doctor is coming shortly. He is authorized to spend the night with you." He made a military salute and left.

"What did I tell you," Tom said. "We get it."

"Yes," I said, "it's a rotten deal for the kid."

I said that to be decent but I didn't like the kid. His face was too thin and fear and suffering had disfigured it, twisting all his features. Three days before he was a smart sort of kid, not too bad; but now he looked like an old fairy and I thought how he'd never be young again, even if they were to let him go. It wouldn't have been too hard to have a little pity for him but pity disgusts me, or rather it horrifies me. He hadn't said anything more but he had turned grey; his face and hands were both grey. He sat down again and looked at the ground with round eyes. Tom was good hearted, he wanted to take his arm, but the kid tore himself away violently and made a face.

"Let him alone," I said in a low voice, "you can see he's going to blubber."

Tom obeyed regretfully; he would have liked to comfort the kid, it would have passed his time and he wouldn't have been tempted to think about himself. But it annoyed me: I'd never thought about death because I never had any reason to, but now the reason was here and there was nothing to do but think about it.

Tom began to talk. "So you think you've knocked guys off, do you?" he asked me. I didn't answer. He began explaining to me that he had knocked off six since the beginning of August; he didn't realize the situation and I could tell he didn't *want* to realize it. I hadn't quite realized it myself, I wondered if it hurt much, I thought of bullets, I imagined their burning hail through my body. All that was beside the real question; but I was calm: we had all night to understand. After a while Tom stopped talking and I watched him out of the corner of my eye; I saw he too had turned grey and he looked rotten; I told myself "Now it starts." It was almost dark, a dim glow filtered through the airholes and the pile of coal and made a big stain beneath the spot of sky; I could already see a star through the hole in the ceiling: the night would be pure and icy.

The door opened and two guards came in, followed by a blonde man in a tan uniform. He saluted us. "I am the doctor," he said. "I have authorization to help you in these trying hours."

He had an agreeable and distinguished voice. I said, "What do you want here?"

"I am at your disposal. I shall do all I can to make your last moments less difficult."

"What did you come here for? There are others, the hospital's full of them."

"I was sent here," he answered with a vague look. "Ah! Would you like to smoke?" he added hurriedly, "I have cigarettes and even cigars."

He offered us English cigarettes and *puros,* but we refused. I looked him in the eyes and he seemed irritated. I said to him, "You aren't here on an errand of mercy. Besides, I know you. I saw you with the fascists in the barracks yard the day I was arrested."

I was going to continue, but something surprising suddenly happened to me; the presence of this doctor no longer interested me. Generally when I'm on somebody I don't let go. But the desire to talk left me completely; I shrugged and turned my eyes away. A little later I raised my head; he was watching me curiously. The guards were sitting on a mat. Pedro, the tall thin one, was twiddling his thumbs, the other shook his head from time to time to keep from falling asleep.

"Do you want a light?" Pedro suddenly asked the doctor. The other nodded "Yes": I think he was about as smart as a log, but he surely wasn't bad. Looking in his cold blue eyes it seemed to me that his only sin was lack of imagination. Pedro went out and came back with an oil lamp which he set on the corner of the bench. It gave a bad light but it was better than nothing: they had left us in the dark the night before. For a long time I watched the circle of light the lamp made on the ceiling. I was fascinated. Then suddenly I woke up, the circle of light disappeared and I felt myself crushed under an enormous weight. It was not the thought of death or fear; it was nameless. My cheeks burned and my head ached.

I shook myself and looked at my two friends. Tom had hidden his face in his hands. I could only see the fat white nape of his neck. Little Juan was the worst; his mouth was open and his nostrils trembled. The doctor went to him and put his hand on his shoulder to comfort him, but his eyes stayed cold. Then I saw the Belgian's hand drop stealthily along Juan's arm, down to the wrist. Juan paid no attention. The Belgian took his wrist between three fingers, distractedly, the same time drawing back a little and turning his back to me. But I leaned backward and saw him take a watch from his pocket and look at it for a moment, never letting go of the wrist. After a minute he let the hand fall inert and went and leaned his back against the wall, then, as if he suddenly remembered something very important which had to be jotted down on the spot, he took a notebook from his pocket and wrote a few lines. "Bastard," I thought angrily, "let him come and take my pulse. I'll shove my fist in his rotten face."

He didn't come but I felt him watching me. I raised my head and returned his look. Impersonally, he said to me, "Doesn't it seem cold to you here?" He looked cold, he was blue.

"I'm not cold," I told him.

He never took his hard eyes off me. Suddenly I understood and my hands went to my face: I was drenched in sweat. In this cellar, in the midst of winter, in the midst of drafts, I was sweating. I ran my hands through my hair, gummed together with perspiration; at the same time I saw my shirt was damp and sticking to my skin: I had been dripping for an hour and hadn't felt it. But that swine of a Belgian hadn't missed a thing; he had seen the drops rolling down my cheeks and thought: this is the manifestation of an almost pathological state of terror; and he had felt normal and proud of being alive because he was cold. I wanted to stand up and smash his face but no sooner had I made the slightest gesture than my rage and shame were wiped out; I fell back on the bench with indifference.

I satisfied myself by rubbing my neck with my handkerchief because now I felt the sweat dropping from my hair onto my neck and it was unpleasant. I soon gave up rubbing, it was useless; my handkerchief was already soaked and I was still sweating. My buttocks were sweating too and my damp trousers were glued to the bench.

Suddenly Juan spoke. "You're a doctor?"

"Yes," the Belgian said.

"Does it hurt . . . very long?"

"Huh? When . . .? Oh, no," the Belgian said paternally. "Not at all. It's over quickly." He acted as though he were calming a cash customer.

"But I . . . they told me . . . sometimes they have to fire twice."

"Sometimes," the Belgian said, nodding. "It may happen that the first volley reaches no vital organs."

"Then they have to reload their rifles and aim all over again?" He thought for a moment and then added hoarsely, "That takes time!"

He had a terrible fear of suffering, it was all he thought about: it was his age. I never thought much about it and it wasn't fear of suffering that made me sweat.

I got up and walked to the pile of coal dust. Tom jumped up and threw me a hateful look: I had annoyed him because my shoes squeaked. I wondered if my face looked as frightened as his: I saw he was sweating too. The sky was superb, no light filtered into the dark corner and I had only to raise my head to see the Big Dipper. But it wasn't like it had been: the night before I could see a great piece of sky from my monastery cell and each hour of the day brought me a different memory. Morning, when the sky was a hard, light blue, I thought of beaches on the Atlantic; at noon I saw the sun and I remembered a bar in Seville where I drank *manzanilla* and ate olives and anchovies; afternoons I was in the shade and I thought of the deep shadow which spreads over half a bull-ring leaving the other half shimmering in sunlight; it was really hard to see the whole world reflected in the sky like that. But now I could watch the sky as much as I pleased, it no longer evoked anything in me. I liked that better. I came back and sat near Tom. A long moment passed.

Tom began speaking in a low voice. He had to talk, without that he wouldn't have been able to recognize himself in his own mind. I thought he was talking to me but he wasn't looking at me. He was undoubtedly afraid to see me as I was, grey and sweating: we were alike and worse than mirrors of each other. He watched the Belgian, the living.

"Do you understand?" he said. "I don't understand."

I began to speak in a low voice too. I watched the Belgian. "Why? What's the matter?"

"Something is going to happen to us that I can't understand."

There was a strange smell about Tom. It seemed to me I was more sensitive than usual to odors. I grinned. "You'll understand in a while."

"It isn't clear," he said obstinately. "I want to be brave but first I have to know . . . Listen, they're going to take us into the court-yard. Good. They're going to stand up in front of us. How many?"

"I don't know. Five or eight. Not more."

"All right. There'll be eight. Someone'll holler 'aim!' and I'll see eight rifles looking at me. I'll think how I'd like to get inside the wall, I'll push against it with my back . . . with every ounce of strength I have, but the wall will stay, like in a nightmare. I can imagine all that. If you only knew how well I can imagine it."

"All right, all right!" I said, "I can imagine it too."

"It must hurt like hell. You know, they aim at the eyes and the mouth to disfigure you," he added mechanically. "I can feel the wounds already; I've had pains in my head and in my neck for the past hour. Not real pains. Worse. This is what I'm going to feel tomorrow morning. And then what?"

I well understood what he meant but I didn't want to act as if I did. I had pains too, pains in my body like a crowd of tiny scars. I couldn't get used to it. But I was like him, I attached no importance to it. "After," I said, "you'll be pushing up daisies."

He began to talk to himself: he never stopped watching the Belgian. The Belgian didn't seem to be listening. I knew what he had come to do; he wasn't interested in what we thought; he came to watch our bodies, bodies dying in agony while yet alive.

"It's like a nightmare," Tom was saying. "You want to think of something, you always have the impression that it's all right, that you're going to understand and then it slips, it escapes you and fades away. I tell myself there will be nothing afterwards. But I don't understand what it means. Sometimes I almost can . . . and then it fades away and I start thinking about the pains again, bullets, explosions. I'm a materialist, I swear it to you; I'm not going crazy. But something's the matter. I see my corpse; that's not hard but I'*m* the one who sees it, with *my* eyes. I've got to think . . . think that I won't see anything anymore and the world will go on for the others. We aren't made to think that, Pablo. Believe me: I've already stayed up a whole night waiting for something. But this isn't the same: this will creep up behind us, Pablo, and we won't be able to prepare for it."

"Shut up," I said, "Do you want me to call a priest?"

He didn't answer. I had already noticed he had the tendency to act like a prophet and call me Pablo, speaking in a toneless voice. I didn't like that: but it seems all the Irish are that way. I had the vague impression he smelled of urine. Fundamentally, I hadn't much sympathy for Tom and I didn't see why, under the pretext of dying together, I should have any more. It would have been different with some others. With Ramon Gris, for example. But I felt alone between Tom and Juan. I liked that better, anyhow: with Ramon I might have been more deeply moved. But I was terribly hard just then and I wanted to stay hard.

He kept on chewing his words, with something like distraction. He certainly talked to keep himself from thinking. He smelled of urine like an old prostate case. Naturally, I agreed with him, I could have said everything he said: it isn't *natural* to die. And since I was going to die, nothing seemed natural to me, not this pile of coal dust, or the bench, or Pedro's ugly face. Only it didn't please me to think the same things as Tom. And I knew that, all through the night, every five minutes, we would keep on thinking things at the same time. I looked at him sideways and for the first time he seemed strange to me: he wore death on his face. My pride was wounded: for the past twenty-four hours I had lived next to Tom, I had listened to him, I had spoken to him and I knew we had nothing in common. And now we looked as much alike as twin brothers, simply because we were going to die together. Tom took my hand without looking at me.

"Pablo, I wonder . . . I wonder if it's really true that everything ends."

I took my hand away and said, "Look between your feet, you pig."

There was a big puddle between his feet and drops fell from his pants-leg.

"What is it?" he asked frightened.

"You're pissing in your pants," I told him.

"It isn't true," he said furiously. "I'm not pissing. I don't feel anything."

The Belgian approached us. He asked with false solicitude, "Do you feel ill?"

Tom did not answer. The Belgian looked at the puddle and said nothing.

"I don't know what it is," Tom said ferociously. "But I'm not afraid. I swear I'm not afraid."

The Belgian did not answer. Tom got up and went to piss in a corner. He came back buttoning his fly, and sat down without a word. The Belgian was taking notes.

All three of us watched him because he was alive. He had the motions of a living human being, the cares of a living human being; he shivered in the cellar the way the living are supposed to shiver; he had an obedient, well-fed body. The rest of us hardly felt ours—not in the same way anyhow. I wanted to feel my pants between my legs but I didn't dare; I watched the Belgian, balancing on his legs, master of his muscles, someone who could think about tomorrow. There we were, three bloodless shadows; we watched him and we sucked his life like vampires.

Finally he went over to little Juan. Did he want to feel his neck for some professional motive or was he obeying an impulse of charity? If he was acting by charity it was the only time during the whole night.

He caressed Juan's head and neck. The kid let himself be handled, his eyes never leaving him, then suddenly, he seized the hand and looked at it strangely. He held the Belgian's hand between his own two hands and there was nothing pleasant about them, two grey pincers gripping his fat and reddish hand. I suspected what was going to happen and Tom must have suspected it too: but the Belgian didn't see a thing, he smiled paternally. After a moment the kid brought the fat red hand to his mouth and tried to bite it. The Belgian pulled away quickly and stumbled back against the wall. For a second he looked at us with horror, he must have suddenly understood that we were not men like him. I began to laugh and one of the guards jumped up. The other was asleep, his wide open eyes were blank.

I felt relaxed and over-excited at the same time. I didn't want to think any more about what would happen at dawn, at death. It made no sense. I only found words or emptiness. But as soon as I tried to think of anything else I saw rifle barrels pointing at me. Perhaps I lived through my execution twenty times; once I even thought it was for good: I must have slept a minute. They were dragging me to the wall and I was struggling; I was asking for mercy. I woke up with a start and looked at the Belgian: I was afraid I might have cried out in my sleep. But he was stroking his moustache, he hadn't noticed anything. If I had wanted to, I think I could have slept a while; I had been awake for forty-eight hours. I was at the end of my rope. But I didn't want to lose two hours of life: they would come to wake me up at dawn, I would follow them, stupefied with sleep and I would have croaked without so much as an "Oof!"; I didn't want that, I didn't want to die like an animal, I wanted to understand. Then I was afraid of having nightmares. I got up, walked back and forth, and, to change my ideas, I began to think about my past life. A crowd of memories came back to me pell-mell. There were good and bad ones—or at least I called them that *before*. There were faces and incidents. I saw the face of a little *novillero* who was gored in Valencia during the *Feria*, the face of one of my uncles, the face of Ramon Gris. I remembered my whole life: how I was out of work for three months in 1926, how I almost starved to death. I remembered a night I spent on a bench in Granada: I hadn't eaten for three days. I was angry, I didn't want to die. That made me smile. How madly I ran after happiness, after women, after liberty. Why? I wanted to free Spain, I admired Pi y Margall, I joined the anarchist movement, I spoke in public meetings: I took everything as seriously as if I were immortal.

At that moment I felt that I had my whole life in front of me, and I thought, "It's a damned lie." It was worth nothing because it was finished. I wondered how I'd been able to walk, to laugh with the girls: I wouldn't have moved so much as my little finger if I had only imagined I would die like this. My life was in front of me, shut, closed, like a bag and yet everything inside of it was unfinished. For an instant I tried to judge it. I wanted to tell myself, this is a beautiful life. But I couldn't pass judgment on it; it was only a sketch; I had spent my time counterfeiting eternity, I had understood nothing. I missed nothing: there were so many things I could have missed, the taste of *manzanilla* or the baths I took in summer in a little creek near Cadiz; but death had disenchanted everything.

The Belgian suddenly had a bright idea. "My friends," he told us, "I will undertake—if the military administration will allow it—to send a message for you, a souvenir to those who love you . . ."

Tom mumbled, "I don't have anybody."

I said nothing. Tom waited an instant then looked at me with curiosity. "You don't have anything to say to Concha?"

"No."

I hated this tender complicity: it was my own fault, I had talked about Concha the night before, I should have controlled myself. I was with her for a year. Last night I would have given an arm to see her again for five minutes. That was why I talked about her, it was stronger than I was. Now I had no more desire to see her, I had nothing more to say to her. I would not even have wanted to hold her in my arms: my body filled me with horror because it was grey and sweating—and I wasn't sure that her body didn't fill me with horror. Concha would cry when she found out I was dead, she would have no taste for life for months afterwards. But I was still the one who was going to die. I thought of her soft, beautiful eyes. When she looked at me something passed from her to me. But I knew it was over: if she looked at me *now* the look would stay in her eyes, it wouldn't reach me. I was alone.

Tom was alone too but not in the same way. Sitting cross-legged, he had begun to stare at the bench with a sort of smile, he looked amazed. He put out his hand and touched the wood cautiously as if he were afraid of breaking something, then drew back his hand quickly and shuddered. If I had been Tom I wouldn't have amused myself by touching the bench; this was some more Irish nonsense, but I too found that objects had a funny look: they were more obliterated, less dense than usual. It was enough for me to look at the bench, the lamp, the pile of coal dust, to feel that I was going to die. Naturally I couldn't think clearly about my death but I saw it everywhere, on things, in the way things fell back and kept their distance, discreetly, as people who speak quietly at the bedside of a dying man. It was *his* death which Tom had just touched on the bench.

In the state I was in, if someone had come and told me I could go home quietly, that they would leave me my life whole, it would have left me cold: several hours or several years of waiting is all the same when you have lost the illusion of being eternal. I clung to nothing, in a way I was calm. But it was a horrible calm—because of my body; my body, I saw with its eyes, I heard with its ears, but it was no longer me; it sweated and trembled by itself and I didn't recognize it any more. I had to touch it and look at it to find out what was happening, as if it were the body of someone else. At times I could still feel it, I felt sinkings, and fallings, as when you're in a plane taking a nosedive, or I felt my heart beating. But that didn't reassure me. Everything that came from my body was all cock-eyed. Most of the time it was quiet and I felt no more than a sort of weight, a filthy presence against me; I had the impression of being tied to an enormous vermin. Once I felt my pants and I felt they were damp; I didn't know whether it was sweat or urine, but I went to piss on the coal pile as a precaution.

The Belgian took out his watch, looked at it. He said, "It's three-thirty."

Bastard! He must have done it on purpose. Tom jumped; we

hadn't noticed time was running out; night surrounded us like a shapeless, somber mass, I couldn't even remember that it had begun.

Little Juan began to cry. He wrung his hands, pleaded, "I don't want to die. I don't want to die."

He ran across the whole cellar waving his arms in the air, then fell sobbing on one of the mats. Tom watched him with mournful eyes, without the slightest desire to console him. Because it wasn't worth the trouble: the kid made more noise than we did, but he was less touched: he was like a sick man who defends himself against his illness by fever. It's much more serious when there isn't any fever.

He wept: I could clearly see he was pitying himself; he wasn't thinking about death. For one second, one single second, I wanted to weep myself, to weep with pity for myself. But the opposite happened: I glanced at the kid, I saw his thin sobbing shoulders and I felt inhuman: I could pity neither the others nor myself. I said to myself, "I want to die cleanly."

Tom had gotten up, he placed himself just under the round opening and began to watch for daylight. I was determined to die cleanly and I only thought of that. But ever since the doctor told us the time, I felt time flying, flowing away drop by drop.

It was still dark when I heard Tom's voice: "Do you hear them?"

Men were marching in the courtyard.

"Yes."

"What the hell are they doing? They can't shoot in the dark."

After a while we heard no more. I said to Tom, "It's day."

Pedro got up, yawning, and came to blow out the lamp. He said to his buddy, "Cold as hell."

The cellar was all grey. We heard shots in the distance.

"It's starting," I told Tom. "They must do it in the court in the rear."

Tom asked the doctor for a cigarette. I didn't want one; I didn't want cigarettes or alcohol. From that moment on they didn't stop firing.

"Do you realize what's happening?" Tom said.

He wanted to add something but kept quiet, watching the door. The door opened and a lieutenant came in with four soldiers. Tom dropped his cigarette.

"Steinbock?"

Tom didn't answer. Pedro pointed him out.

"Juan Mirbal?"

"On the mat."

"Get up," the lieutenant said.

Juan did not move. Two soldiers took him under the arms and

set him on his feet. But he fell as soon as they released him.

The soldiers hesitated.

"He's not the first sick one," said the lieutenant. "You two carry him; they'll fix it up down there."

He turned to Tom. "Let's go."

Tom went out between two soldiers. Two others followed, carrying the kid by the armpits. He hadn't fainted; his eyes were wide open and tears ran down his cheeks. When I wanted to go out the lieutenant stopped me.

"You Ibbieta?"

"Yes."

"You wait here; they'll come for you later."

They left. The Belgian and the two jailers left too, I was alone. I did not understand what was happening to me but I would have liked it better if they had gotten it over with right away. I heard shots at almost regular intervals; I shook with each one of them. I wanted to scream and tear out my hair. But I gritted my teeth and pushed my hands in my pockets because I wanted to stay clean.

After an hour they came to get me and led me to the first floor, to a small room that smelt of cigars and where the heat was stifling. There were two officers sitting smoking in the armchairs, papers on their knees.

"You're Ibbieta?"

"Yes."

"Where is Ramon Gris?"

"I don't know."

The one questioning me was short and fat. His eyes were hard behind his glasses. He said to me, "Come here."

I went to him. He got up and took my arms, staring at me with a look that should have pushed me into the earth. At the same time he pinched my biceps with all his might. It wasn't to hurt me, it was only a game: he wanted to dominate me. He also thought he had to blow his stinking breath square in my face. We stayed for a moment like that, and I almost felt like laughing. It takes a lot to intimidate a man who is going to die; it didn't work. He pushed me back violently and sat down again. He said, "It's his life against yours. You can have yours if you tell us where he is."

These men dolled up with their riding crops and boots were still going to die. A little later than I, but not too much. They busied themselves looking for names in their crumpled papers, they ran after other men to imprison or suppress them; they had opinions on the future of Spain and on other subjects. Their little activities seemed shocking and burlesqued to me; I couldn't put myself in their place, I thought they were insane. The little man was still looking at me, whipping his boots with the riding crop. All his gestures were calculated to give him the look of a live and ferocious beast.

"So? You understand?"

"I don't know where Gris is," I answered. "I thought he was in Madrid."

The other officer raised his pale hand indolently. This indolence was also calculated. I saw through all their little schemes and I was stupefied to find there were men who amused themselves that way.

"You have a quarter of an hour to think it over," he said slowly. "Take him to the laundry, bring him back in fifteen minutes. If he still refuses he will be executed on the spot."

They knew what they were doing: I had passed the night in waiting; then they had made me wait an hour in the cellar while they shot Tom and Juan and now they were locking me up in the laundry; they must have prepared their game the night before. They told themselves that nerves eventually wear out and they hoped to get me that way.

They were badly mistaken. In the laundry I sat on a stool because I felt very weak and I began to think. But not about their proposition. Of course I knew where Gris was; he was hiding with his cousins, four kilometers from the city. I also knew that I would not reveal his hiding place unless they tortured me (but they didn't seem to be thinking about that). All that was perfectly regulated, definite and in no way interested me. Only I would have liked to understand the reasons for my conduct. I would rather die than give up Gris. Why? I didn't like Ramon Gris any more. My friendship for him had died a little while before dawn at the same time as my love for Concha, at the same time as my desire to live. Undoubtedly I thought highly of him: he was tough. But it was not for this reason that I consented to die in his place; his life had no more value than mine; no life had value. They were going to slap a man up against a wall and shoot at him until he died, whether it was I or Gris or somebody else made no difference. I knew he was more useful than I to the cause of Spain but I thought to hell with Spain and anarchy; nothing was important. Yet I was there, I could save my skin and give up Gris and I refused to do it. I found that somehow comic; it was obstinacy. I thought, "I must be stubborn!" And a droll sort of gaiety spread over me.

They came for me and brought me back to the two officers. A rat ran out from under my feet and that amused me. I turned to one of the *falangistas* and said, "Did you see the rat?"

He didn't answer. He was very sober, he took himself seriously. I wanted to laugh but I held myself back because I was afraid that once I got started I wouldn't be able to stop. The *falangista* had a moustache. I said to him again, "You ought to shave off your moustache, idiot." I thought it funny that he would let the hairs of his living being invade his face. He kicked me without great conviction and I kept quiet.

"Well," said the fat officer, "have you thought about it?"

I looked at them with curiosity, as insects of a very rare species. I told them, "I know where he is. He is hidden in the cemetery. In a vault or in the gravediggers' shack."

It was a farce. I wanted to see them stand up, buckle their belts and give orders busily.

They jumped to their feet. "Let's go. Molés, go get fifteen men from Lieutenant Lopez. You," the fat man said, "I'll let you off if you're telling the truth, but it'll cost you plenty if you're making monkeys out of us."

They left in a great clatter and I waited peacefully under the guard of *falangistas*. From time to time I smiled, thinking about the spectacle they would make. I felt stunned and malicious. I imagined them lifting up tombstones, opening the doors of the vaults one by one. I represented this situation to myself as if I had been someone else: this prisoner obstinately playing the hero, these grim *falangistas* with their moustaches and their men in uniform running among the graves; it was irresistibly funny. After half an hour the little fat man came back alone. I thought he had come to give the orders to excute me. The others must have stayed in the cemetery.

The officer looked at me. He didn't look at all sheepish. "Take him into the big courtyard with the others," he said. "After the military operations a regular court will decide what happens to him."

"Then they're not . . . not going to shoot me? . . ."

"Not now, anyway. What happens afterwards is none of my business."

I still didn't understand. I asked, "But why?"

He shrugged his shoulders without answering and the soldiers took me away. In the big courtyard there were about a hundred prisoners, women, children and a few old men. I began walking around the central grass-plot, I was stupefied. At noon they let us eat in the mess hall. Two or three people questioned me. I must have known them, but I didn't answer: I didn't even know where I was.

Around evening they pushed about ten new prisoners into the court. I recognized Garcia, the baker. He said, "What damned luck you have! I didn't think I'd see you alive."

"They sentenced me to death," I said, "and then they changed their minds, I don't know why."

"They arrested me at two o'clock," Garcia said.

"Why?" Garcia had nothing to do with politics.

"I don't know," he said. "They arrest everybody who doesn't think the way they do." He lowered his voice. "They got Gris."

I began to tremble. "When?"

"This morning. He messed it up. He left his cousin's on Tuesday because they had an argument. There were plenty of people to hide him but he didn't want to owe anything to anybody. He said, 'I'd go hide in Ibbieta's place, but they got him, so I'll go hide in the cemetery.'"

"In the cemetery?"

"Yes. What a fool. Of course they went by there this morning, that was sure to happen. They found him in the gravediggers' shack. He shot at them and they got him."

"In the cemetery!"

Everything began to spin and I found myself sitting on the ground: I laughed so hard I cried.

Alberto Moravia

BITTER HONEYMOON

They had chosen Anacapri for their honeymoon because Giacomo had been there a few months before and wanted to go back, taking his bride with him. His previous visit had been in the spring, and he remembered the clear, crisp air and the flowers alive with the hum of thousands of insects in the golden glow of the sun. But this time, immediately upon their arrival, everything seemed very different. The sultry dog-days of mid-August were upon them and steaming humidity overclouded the sky. Even on the heights of Anacapri, there was no trace of the crisp air, of flowers or the violet sea whose praises Giacomo had sung. The paths winding through the fields were covered with a layer of yellow dust, accumulated in the course of four months without rain, in which even gliding lizards left traces of their passage. Long before autumn was due, the leaves had begun to turn red and brown, and occasional whole trees had withered away for lack of water. Dust particles filled the motionless air and made the nostrils quiver, and the odors of meadows and sea had given way to those of scorched stones and dried dung. The water, which in the spring had taken its color from what seemed to be banks of violets floating just below the surface, was now a gray mass reflecting the melancholy, dazzling light brought by the *scirocco* which infested the sky.

"I don't think it's the least bit beautiful," Simona said on the day after their arrival, as they started along the path to the lighthouse. "I don't like it—no, not at all."

Giacomo, following several steps behind, did not answer. She

Translated by Frances Frenaye. Reprinted from *Bitter Honeymoon* by Alberto Moravia, by permission of Farrar, Straus & Giroux, Inc. Copyright © 1956 by Valentino Bompiani & Co., and published in England by Martin Secker & Warburg Limited.

had spoken in this plaintive and discontented tone of voice ever since they had emerged from their civil marriage in Rome, and he suspected that her prolonged ill-humor mingled with an apparent physical repulsion, was not connected so much with the place as with his own person. She was complaining about Anacapri because she was not aware that her fundamental dissatisfaction was with her husband. Theirs was a love match to be sure, but one based rather on the will to love than on genuine feeling. There was good reason for his presentiment of trouble when, as he slipped the ring on her finger, he had read a flicker of regret and embarrassment on her face; for on their first night at Anacapri she had begged off, on the plea of fatigue and seasickness, from giving herself to him. On this, the second day of their marriage, she was just as much of a virgin as she had been before.

As she trudged wearily along, with a bag slung over one shoulder, between the dusty hedges, Giacomo looked at her with almost sorrowful intensity, hoping to take possession of her with a single piercing glance, as he had so often done with other women. But, as he realized right away, the piercing quality was lacking; his eyes fell with analytical affection upon her, but there was in them none of the transfiguring power of real passion. Although Simona was not tall, she had childishly long legs with slender thighs, rising to an indentation, almost a cleft at either side, visible under her shorts, where they were joined to the body. The whiteness of her legs was chaste, shiny and cold, she had a narrow waist and hips, and her only womanly feature, revealed when she turned around to speak to him, was the fullness of her low-swung breasts, which seemed like extraneous and burdensome weights, unsuited to her delicate frame. Similarly her thick, blond hair, although it was cut short, hung heavily over her neck. All of a sudden, as if she felt that she was being watched, she wheeled around and asked: "Why do you make me walk ahead of you?"

Giacomo saw the childishly innocent expression of her big blue eyes, her small, tilted nose and equally childishly rolled-back upper lip. Her face, too, he thought to himself, was a stranger to him, untouched by love.

"I'll go ahead, if you like," he said with resignation.

And he went by her, deliberately brushing her breast with his elbow to test his own desire. Then they went on walking, he ahead and she behind. The path wound about the summit of Monte Solaro, running along a wall of mossy stones with no masonry to hold them together and rows of vines strung out above them. On the other side there was a sheer descent, through uninhabited stretches of vineyard and olive grove, to the mist-covered gray sea. Only a solitary pine tree, halfway down the mountain, with its green crest floating in the air, recalled the idyllic purity of the landscape in its better days. Simona walked very slowly, lagging farther behind at every step. Finally she came to a halt and asked: "Have we far to go?"

"We've only just started," Giacomo said lightly. "At least an hour more."

"I can't bear it," she said ill-humoredly, looking at him as if she hoped he would propose giving up the walk altogether. He went back to her and put her arm around his waist.

"You can't bear the exertion or you can't bear me?"

"What do you mean, silly?" she countered with unexpected feeling. "I can't bear to go on walking, of course."

"Give me a kiss."

She administered a rapid peck on his cheek.

"It's so hot . . ." she murmured. "I wish we could go home."

"We must get to the lighthouse," Giacomo answered. "What's the point of going back? . . . We'll have a swim as soon as we arrive. It's a wonderful place, and the lighthouse is all pink and white. . . . Don't you want to see it?"

"Yes; but I'd like to fly there instead of walking."

"Let's talk," he suggested. "That way you won't notice the distance."

"But I have nothing to say," she protested, almost with tears in her voice.

Giacomo hesitated for a moment before replying:

"You know so much poetry by heart. Recite a poem, and I'll listen; then before you know it, we'll be there."

He could see that he had hit home, for she had a truly extraordinary memory for verse.

"What shall I recite?" she asked with childish vanity.

"A canto from Dante."

"Which one?"

"The third canto of the *Inferno*," Giacomo said at random. Somewhat consoled, Simona walked on, once more ahead of him, beginning to recite:

> "Per me si va nella città dolente:
> per me si va nell'eterno dolore:
> per me si va tra la perduta gente . . ."

She recited mechanically and with as little expression as a schoolgirl, breathing hard because of the double effort required of her. As she walked doggedly along, she paused at the end of every line, without paying any attention to syntax or meaning, like a schoolgirl endowed with zeal rather than intelligence. Every now and then she turned appealingly around and shot him a fleeting look, yes, exactly like a schoolgirl, with the blue-and-white cap perched on her blond hair. After they had gone some way they reached a wall built all around a large villa. The wall was covered with ivy, and leafy oak branches grew out over it.

" '*E caddi, come l'uom, cui sonno piglia,*" Simona said, winding up the third canto; then she turned around and asked: "Whose place is this?"

"It belonged to Axel Munthe," Giacomo answered; "but he's dead now."

"And what sort of a fellow was he?"

"A very shrewd sort indeed," said Giacomo. And, in order to amuse her, he added: "He was a doctor very fashionable in Rome at the turn of the century. If you'd like to know more about him, there's a story I've been told is absolutely true. . . . Would you like to hear it?"

"Yes; do tell me."

"Once a beautiful and frivolous society woman came to him with all sorts of imaginary ailments. Munthe listened patiently, examined her, and when he saw that there was nothing wrong, said: 'I know a sure cure, but you must do exactly what I say. . . . Go and look out of that open window and lean your elbows on the sill.' She obeyed, and Munthe went after her and gave her a terrific kick in the rear. Then he escorted her to the door and said: 'Three times a week, and in a few months you'll be quite all right.' "

Simona failed to laugh, and after a moment she said bitterly, looking at the wall: "That would be the cure for me."

Giacomo was struck by her mournful tone of voice.

"Why do you say that?" he asked, coming up to her. "What's come into your head?"

"It's true. . . . I'm slightly mad, and you ought to treat me exactly that way."

"What are you talking about?"

"About what happened last night," she said with startling frankness.

"But last night you were tired and seasick."

"That wasn't it at all. I'm never seasick, and I wasn't tired, either. I was afraid, that's all."

"Afraid of me?"

"No; afraid of the whole idea."

They walked on in silence. The wall curved, following the path and hanging slightly over, as if it could hardly contain the oak trees behind it. Then it came to an end, and in front of them lay a grassy plateau, below which the mountainside fell abruptly down to the arid and lonely promontories of Rio. The plateau was covered with asphodels, whose pyramidal flowers were of a dusty rose, almost gray in color. Giacomo picked some and handed them to his wife, saying: "Look. How beautiful . . ."

She raised them to her nose, like a young girl on her way to the altar, inhaling the fragrance of a lily. Perhaps she was conscious of her virginal air, for she pressed close to him, in something like an embrace, and whispered into one ear: "Don't believe what I just told you. . . . I wasn't afraid. . . . I'll just have to get used to the idea. . . . Tonight . . ."

"Tonight?" he repeated.

"You're so very dear to me," she murmured painfully, adding a strictly conventional phrase, which she seemed to have learned for the occasion, "Tonight I'll be yours."

She said these last words hurriedly, as if she were afraid of the conventionality rather than the substance of them, and planted a hasty kiss on his cheek. It was the first time that she had ever told Giacomo that he was dear to her or anything like it, and he was tempted to take her in his arms. But she said in a loud voice: "Look! What's that down there on the sea?" And at the same time she eluded his grasp.

Giacomo looked in the direction at which she was pointing and saw a solitary sail emerging from the mist that hung over the water.

"A boat," he said testily.

She started walking again, at a quickened pace, as if she were afraid that he might try once more to embrace her. And as he saw her escape him he had a recurrent feeling of impotence, because he could not take immediate possession of his beloved.

"You won't do that to me tonight," he muttered between clenched teeth as he caught up with her.

And she answered, lowering her head without looking around: "It will be different tonight. . . ."

It was really hot—there was no doubt about that—and in the heavy air all round them there seemed to Giacomo to reside the same obstacle, the same impossibility that bogged down his relationship with his wife: the impossibility of a rainfall that would clear the air, the impossibility of love. He had a senation of something like panic, when looking at her again he felt that his will to love was purely intellectual and did not involve his senses. Her figure was outlined quite precisely before him, but there was none of the halo around it in which love usually envelops the loved one's person. Impulsively he said: "Perhaps you shouldn't have married me."

Simona seemed to accept this statement as a basis for discussion, as if she had had the same thought without daring to come out with it.

"Why?" she asked.

Giacomo wanted to answer, "Because we don't really love each other," but although this was the thought in his mind, he expressed it in an entirely different manner. Simona was a Communist and had a job at Party headquarters. Giacomo was not a Communist at all; he claimed to attach no importance to his wife's political ideas, but they had a way of cropping up at the most unexpected moments as underlying motives for disagreement. And now he was astonished to hear himself say: "Because there is too great a difference of ideas between us."

"What sort of ideas do you mean?"

"Political ideas."

He realized, then, why her standoffishness had caused him to bring politics into the picture; it was with the hope of arousing a reaction to a point on which he knew her to be sensitive. And indeed she answered immediately: "That's not so. The truth is that I have certain ideas and you have none at all."

As soon as politics came up she assumed a self-sufficient, pedantic manner, quite the opposite of childish, which always threatened to infuriate him. He asked himself in all conscience whether his irritation stemmed from some latent anti-Communist feeling within himself, but quickly set his mind at rest on this score. He had no interest in politics whatsoever, and the only thing that bothered him was the fact that his wife did have such an interest.

"Well, whether or not it's a question of ideas," he said dryly, "there is *something* between us."

"What is it, then?"

"I don't know, but I can feel it."

After a second she said in the same irritating tone of voice: "I know quite well. It *is* a question of ideas. But I hope that some day you'll see things the way I do."

"Never."

"Why never?"

"I've told you so many times before. . . . First, because I don't want to be involved in politics of any kind, and, second, because I'm too much of an individualist."

Simona made no reply, but in such cases her silence was direr than spoken disapproval. Giacomo was overcome by a wave of sudden anger. He overtook her and seized her arm.

"All this is going to have very serious consequences some day," he shouted. "For instance, if a Communist government comes to power, and I say something against it, you'll inform on me."

"Why should you say anything against it?" she retorted. "You just said that you don't want to be involved in politics of any kind."

"Anything can happen."

"And then the Communists aren't in power. . . . Why worry about a situation that doesn't exist?"

It was true then, he thought to himself, since she didn't deny it, that she would inform on him. He gripped her arm tighter, almost wishing to hurt her.

"The truth is that you don't love me," he said.

"I wouldn't have married you except for love," she said clearly, and she looked straight at him, with her lower lip trembling. Her voice filled Giacomo with tenderness, and he drew her to him and kissed her. Simona was visibly affected by the kiss; her nostrils stiffened and she breathed hard, and although her arms hung down at her sides, she pressed her body against his.

"My spy," he said, drawing away and stroking her face. "My little spy."

"Why do you call me spy?" she asked, taking immediate offense.

"I was joking."

They walked on, but as he followed her Giacomo wondered whether he had meant the word as a joke after all. And what about his anger? Was that a joke too? He didn't know how he could have given way to such unreasonable anger and have made such even more unreasonable accusations, and yet he dimly understood that they were justified by Simona's behavior. Meanwhile, they had come to the other side of the mountain, and from the highest point of the path they looked down at an immense expanse of air, like a bottomless well. Five minutes later they had a view of all one side of the island, a long, green slope covered with scattered vines and prickly pears, and at the bottom, stretching out into the sea, the chalky promontory on which stood the lighthouse. The sweep of the view was tremendous, and the pink-and-white checked lighthouse, hung between sky and sea, seemed far away and no larger than a man's hand. Simona clapped her hands in delight.

"How perfectly lovely!" she exclaimed.

"I told you it was beautiful, and you wouldn't believe me."

"Forgive me," she said, patting his cheek. "You always know best and I'm very silly."

Before he could control himself, Giacomo said: "Does that go for politics too?"

"No; not for politics. But don't let's talk about that just now."

He was annoyed with himself for having fallen back into an argument, but at the same time he suffered a return of the left-out and jealous feeling that overcame him every time she made a dogmatic, almost religious reference to her political ideas.

"Why shouldn't we talk about it?" he said as gently as he could. "Perhaps if we talked about it, we might understand one another better."

Simona did not reply, and Giacomo walked on after her, in an extremely bad humor. Now he was the one to feel the heaviness and heat of the day, while Simona, intoxicated by the sight of the distant sea, shouted: "Let's run down the rest of the way. I can't wait to get into the water."

With her sling bag bobbing about on her shoulder, she began to run down the path, emitting shrill cries of joy. Giacomo saw that she was throwing her legs in all directions like an untrained colt. Suddenly the thought, "Tonight she'll be mine" floated through his head and quieted him. What could be the importance of belonging to a political party in comparison to that of the act of love, so ageless and so very human? Men had possessed women long before the existence of political parties or religions. And he was sure that in the moment when he possessed Simona he would drive out of her every allegiance except that of her love for him. Strengthened by this thought he ran after her, shouting in his turn: "Wait for me, Simona!"

She stopped to wait, flushed, quivering and bright-eyed. As he caught up with her he said pantingly: "Just now I began to feel very happy. I know that we're going to love one another."

"I know it too," she said, looking at him out of her innocent blue eyes.

Giacomo put one arm around her waist, catching her hand in his and compelling her to throw it over his shoulders. They walked on in this fashion, but Simona's eyes remained set on the water below. Giacomo, on the other hand, could not tear his thoughts away from the body he was holding so tightly. Simona was wearing a skimpy boy's jersey with a patch in the front. And her head was boyish in outline as well, with the unruly short hair falling over her cheeks. Yet her slender waist fitted into the curve of his arm with a womanly softness which seemed to foreshadow the complete surrender promised for the coming night. Suddenly he breathed into her ear: "You'll always be my little friend and comrade."

Simona's mind must have been on the lighthouse, and the word "comrade" came through to her alone, out of context, without the sentimental intonation that gave it Giacomo's intended meaning. For she answered with a smile: "We can't be comrades . . . at least, not until you see things the way I do. . . . But I'll be your wife."

So she was still thinking of the Party, Giacomo said to himself with excusable jealousy. The word "comrade" had for her no tender connotations, but only political significance. The Party continued to have a prior claim to her loyalty.

"I didn't mean it that way," he said disappointedly.

"I'm sorry," she said, hastening to correct herself. "That's what we call each other in the Party."

"I only meant that you'd be my lifelong companion."

"That's true," she said, lowering her head in embarrassment, as if she couldn't really accept the word except politically.

They dropped their arms and walked down the path with no link between them. As they proceeded, the lighthouse seemed to approach them, revealing its tower shape. The water beyond it had a metallic sheen, derived from the direct rays of the sun, while behind them the mountain seemed to grow higher, with a wall of red rock rising above the lower slope which they were now traversing. At the top was a summerhouse with a railing around it, in which they could distinguish two tiny human figures enjoying the view.

"That vantage-point is called La Migliara," Giacomo explained. "A few years ago an Anacapri girl threw herself down the mountain from it, but first she wound her braids around her head and over her eyes so as not to see what she was doing."

Simona tossed a look over her shoulder at the top of the mountain.

"Suicide is all wrong," she said.

Giacomo felt jealousy sting him again.

"Why?" he asked. "Does the Party forbid it?"

"Never mind about the Party." She looked out over the sea and thrust her face and chest forward as if to breathe in the breeze blowing in their direction. "Suicide's all wrong because life is beautiful and it's a joy to be alive."

Again Giacomo didn't really want to get into a political argument; he wanted to make a show of the serenity and detachment which he thoroughly believed were his. But again his annoyance carried him away.

"But T———" (this was the name of a Communist friend they had in common) "committed suicide, didn't he?"

"He did wrong," she said succinctly.

"Why so? He must have had some reason. What do you know?"

"I do know, though," she said obstinately. "He did wrong. It's our duty to live."

"Our duty?"

"Yes; duty."

"Who says so?"

"Nobody. It just is."

"I might just as well say that it's our duty to take our life if we feel it's not worth living. . . . Nobody says so. It just is."

"That's not true," she answered inflexibly. "We were made to live and not to die. . . . Only someone that's sick or in a morbid state of mind can think that life's not worth living."

"So you think that T——— was either sick or in a morbid state of mind, do you?"

"At the moment when he killed himself, yes, I do."

Giacomo was tempted to ask her if this was the Party line, as seemed to him evident from the stubborn note in her voice which annoyed him so greatly, but this time he managed to restrain himself. By now they had reached the bottom of the slope and were crossing a dry, flat area, covered with wood-spurge and prickly pears. Then the land turned into rock and they found themselves before the lighthouse, at the end of the path, which seemed like the end of all human habitation and the beginning of a new and lonely world of colorless chalk and stone. The lighthouse soared up above them as they plunged down among the boulders toward the sea. At a bend, they suddenly came upon a basin of green water, surrounded by rocky black cliffs, eroded by salt. Simona ran down to the cement landing and exclaimed: "Wonderful! Just what I was hoping for! Now we can swim. And we have it all to ourselves. We're quite alone."

She had no sooner spoken these words than a man's voice came out of the rocks: "Simona! What a pleasant surprise."

They turned around, and when a face followed the voice, Simona shouted: "Livio! Hello! Are you here too? What are you doing?"

The young man who emerged from the rocks was short and powerfully built, with broad shoulders. His head contrasted with this athletic body, for it was bald, with only a fringe of hair around the neck, and his flat face had a scholarly expression. The face of a ferret, Giacomo thought, taking an instant dislike to it, not exactly intelligent, but keen and treacherous. He knew the fellow by sight and was aware that he worked in Simona's office. Now Livio came into full view, pulling up his tight, faded red trunks.

"I'm doing the same thing you are, I suppose," he said by way of an answer.

Then Simona said something which gave Giacomo considerable satisfaction.

"That's not very likely. . . . Unless you've just got yourself married. . . . I'm here on my honeymoon. . . . Do you know my husband?"

"Yes; we know each other," Livio said easily, jumping down on to a big square stone and shaking Giacomo's hand so hard that the latter winced with pain as he echoed: "Yes, we've met in Rome." Livio then turned to Simona and added: "I'd heard something to the effect that you were about to marry. But you should have told the comrades. They want to share your joys."

He said all this in a colorless, businesslike voice, but one which was not necessarily devoid of feeling. Giacomo noticed that Simona was smiling and seemed to be waiting for Livio to go on, while Livio stood like a bronze statue on a stone pedestal, with his trunks pulled tightly over his voluminous pubis and all the muscles of his body standing out, and talked down to them. Giacomo felt as if he were somehow left out of their conversation, and drew away, all the while listening intently. They conversed for several minutes without moving, asking one another about various Party workers and where they had spent their vacations.

But Giacomo was struck less by what they said than by the tone in which they said it. What was this tone exactly, and why did it rub him the wrong way? There was a note of complicity in it, he concluded, a reference to some secret bond different from that of either friendship or family. For a moment he wondered if it weren't just what one would find between fellow employees in a bank or government office. But upon reflection, he realized that it was entirely different. It was . . . he searched for some time, groping for an exact definition . . . it was the tone of voice of two monks or two nuns meeting one another. And why then did it rub him the wrong way? Not because he disapproved of Livio's and Simona's political ideas; in the course of a rational discussion he might very well allow that these had some basis. No; there was nothing rational about his hostility; its cause was obscure even to himself and at times it seemed to be one with his jealousy, as if he were afraid that Simona would escape him through her Party connections. As these thoughts ran through his mind, his face grew dark and discontented, so that when Simona joined him, all smiles, a moment later, she exclaimed in surprise: "What's wrong? Why are you unhappy?"

"Nothing . . . It's just the heat."

"Let's go in the water. . . . But first, where can we undress?"

"Just follow me. . . . This way."

He knew the place well, and now led Simona through a narrow passage among the rocks. Behind these rocks they stepped across some other lower ones and then went around a huge mass which sealed off a tiny beach of very fine, black sand at the foot of glistening, black rocky walls around a pool of shallow water filled with black seaweed. The effect was that of a room, with the sky for a ceiling, a watery floor and walls of stone.

"No swimming-bath can match this," Giacomo observed, looking around him.

"At last I can shed my clothes," said Simona with a sigh of relief.

She put her bag down on the sand and bent over to take out her bathing-suit, while, leaning against the rocks, Giacomo stripped himself in a second of his shirt and trousers. The sight of him stark naked caused her to give a nervous laugh.

"This is the sort of place to go swimming with no suits on, isn't it?" she said.

"Unfortunately, one can never manage to be alone," Giacomo replied, thinking of Livio.

He walked, still naked, with bare feet, over the cold sand in her direction, but she did not see him coming because she was pulling her jersey over her head. Her nakedness, he reflected, made her seem more virginal than ever. Her low-swung, round breasts had large rosy nipples, and a look of purity about them, as if they had never been offered to a masculine caress. Indeed, her virginal quality was so overwhelming that Giacomo did not dare press her to him as he had intended, but stood close by while she pulled her head out of the jersey. She shook back her ruffled hair and said in surprise: "What are you doing? Why don't you put on your trunks?"

"I'd like to make love right here and now," said Giacomo.

"On these rocks? Are you mad?"

"No. I'm not mad."

They were facing each other now, he entirely naked and she naked down to the waist. She crossed her arms over her breasts as if to support and protect them and said entreatingly: "Let's wait till tonight. . . . And meanwhile let's go swimming . . . please. . . ."

"Tonight you'll put me off again."

"No; it will be different tonight."

Giacomo walked silently away and proceeded to put on his trunks, while Simona, obviously relieved, hastily donned her two-piece suit. She shouted gaily: "I'm off for a swim! If you love me, you'll follow."

"Let's go in right here," Giacomo suggested.

Simona paused and stuck her white foot into the green and brown seaweed that choked the black water.

"This pool is too murky. . . . It's no more than a puddle. Let's go where we just came from."

"But we shan't be alone."

"Oh, we have plenty of time for that."

They went back to the basin, where Livio was taking a sun-bath on the cement landing, lying as still as if he were dead. Somehow this increased Giacomo's dislike of him. Yes; he was the sort of fellow that goes in for purposeful tanning, and then wanders about showing it off, wearing skimpy trunks designed to exhibit his virility as well. When Livio heard them coming he leaped to his feet and said: "Come on, Simona. Let's dive in and race over to the rock."

"You'll have to give me a handicap of at least a length," she said joyfully, forgetful of her husband.

"I'll give you three lengths, if you say so."

There it was, Giacomo could not help thinking, the same intimate, conspiratorial, clubby, Party manner, that tone of voice in which, despite their marriage, she had never spoken to him, and perhaps never would speak either. Sitting on a flat rock, just above the landing, he watched his wife plunge awkwardly in and then swim like a dark shadow under the green water until she came out, with her blond head dripping.

"That was a real belly-flop," Livio shouted, making a perfect dive to join her. He too swam underwater, but for a longer distance than Simona, so that he came out farther away. Giacomo wondered if this "Party manner" weren't all a product of his imagination, and if there hadn't been in the past some more intimate personal relationship between them. And he realized that this second hypothesis was, on the whole, less disagreeable than the first. Then he said to himself that if he were to mention any such suspicion to Simona she would be outraged and brand it as utterly "bourgeois," not to say "evil-minded and filthy." The moment after he dismissed it as out of the question. No, they were comrades, as she had said, and nothing more. What still puzzled him was why he objected more to their being Party comrades than to their being lovers. With a wavering effort of goodwill, he said to himself that his jealousy was absurd, and he must drive it out of his mind. . . . And all the while he watched the two of them race across the dazzling green water in the direction of a round rock which emerged at the far end of the basin. Livio got there first, and, hoisting himself up on a protruding spur, shouted back at Simona: "I win! You're all washed up!"

"Speak for yourself!" Simona retorted.

This was the sort of joking insult he and Simona should have batted back and forth between them, Giacomo reflected. If they didn't joke that way on their honeymoon, when would they ever do it? He got up decisively, ran several steps along the landing and went in after them. He landed square on his stomach and was infuriated by the pain. After swimming several strokes under water he came up and started toward the rock where Livio and Simona were sitting. They were close together, talking uninterruptedly, with their legs dangling. He didn't relish the sight; in fact, it took away all the pleasure he should have felt from plunging hot and dusty into the cool water. He swam angrily ahead, arrived at the rock breathless and said, hanging on to a ledge: "Do you know, this water's very, very cold."

"It seemed warm to me," said Simona, momentarily interrupting the conversation to shoot him a glance.

"I swam here in April," Livio put in; "it was cold then, I can tell you."

With a curiosity that seemed to Giacomo somewhat flirtatious, Simona asked him: "Were you all alone?"

"No. I came with Nella," Livio answered.

Giacomo was trying to clamber up on the rock, but the only place where he could get a solid grip was the one where Livio and Simona were sitting. They seemed to be oblivious of his struggles, and he preferred not to ask them to move over. Finally, he caught hold of a jutting piece of the rock studded with jagged points, one of which left a pain in the palm of his hand as if it had dug deep into the flesh. Just as he got himself into a sitting position, the other two, with a shout of "Let's race back!" dived into the water, showering him with spray. He looked furiously after them as they raced toward the shore. Only when he had regained his self-control did he plunge in and follow. Simona and Livio were sitting in the shelter of a cliff and Simona was opening a lunch-box that she had taken out of her bag.

"Let's have something to eat," she said to Giacomo as he approached them. "But we must share it with Livio. He says he meant to go back up the mountain, but in this heat it would be too ridiculous."

Without saying a word, Giacomo sat down in the rocks beside them. The contents of the lunch-box turned out to be scanty: some meat sandwiches, two hard-boiled eggs and a bottle of wine.

"Livio will have to be content with very little," Giacomo said gruffly.

"Don't worry," Livio answered gaily. "I'm a very abstemious fellow."

Simona seemed extremely happy as she sat with crossed legs, dividing the lunch. She gave a sandwich to each one of them, bit into her own, and asked Livio:

"Where did you get your tan?"

"On the Tiber," he replied.

"Your whole group is very river-minded, isn't it, Livio?" she asked between one bite and another.

"All except Regina. She scorns the river completely; says it isn't aristocratic enough for her."

The things they talked about were trivial and childish enough, Giacomo reflected. And yet there was a greater intimacy between them than between husband and wife.

"No matter how hard she tries, Regina will never be able to put her background behind her," Simona observed.

"Who is Regina?" asked Giacomo.

"Someone in our outfit . . . the daughter of a wealthy landowner . . . a very fine girl, really," Livio told him. "But wiping out an old trade-mark is no easy matter."

"And in this case, what trade-mark do you mean?"

"The bourgeois trade-mark."

"If you people ever get into power," Giacomo said impulsively, "you'll have to wipe that trade-mark out of millions of people."

"That's exactly what we'll do," Livio said with complete self-confidence. "That's our job, isn't it, Simona?"

Simona's mouth was full, but she nodded assent.

"The Italian bourgeoisie will be a tough nut to crack," Livio went on, "but we'll crack it, even if we have to kill off a large proportion in the process."

"There's a chance you may be killed off yourselves," said Giacomo.

"That's the risk we have to run in our profession," Livio retorted.

Giacomo noticed that Simona did not seem to go along with Livio's ruthlessness; at this last remark she frowned and uttered no word of approval. Livio must have been aware of this, for he brusquely changed the subject.

"Simona, you really should have told us you were getting married, you know. There are some things it's not fair to hide!"

There was a note of tenderness toward Giacomo in Simona's reply.

"We decided from one day to the next. . . . Only the legal witnesses were present. Even our own parents weren't in on it."

"You mean you didn't want them?"

"We didn't want them, and anyhow they might not have come. . . . Giacomo's father and mother didn't want him to marry me."

"Because you're too far to the left, is that it?"

"No," Giacomo interposed. "My people don't go in for politics at all. But my mother had her eyes on a certain girl. . . ."

"They may not go in for politics, as you say," Livio said, after another mouthful, "but there are always political implications. How could it be otherwise? Politics gets into everything these days."

True enough, Giacomo thought to himself. Even into honeymoons and a newly-married couple's first embrace. Then, annoyed at his own train of thought, he held out the hard-boiled eggs to his companions.

"You two eat them," he said. "I'm not hungry."

"Be honest now," Livio said with a look of surprise on his face.

"Why aren't you hungry?" Simona asked him.

"That damned *sciròcco*, I imagine."

Livio looked up at the cloudy sky.

"There'll be a storm before night. I can promise you that," he said.

Livio's conversation was made up of commonplaces and clichés, Giacomo reflected. But Simona seemed to like them. They conveyed more to her than his own attempts to express emotions that were difficult if not impossible to put into words. Meanwhile Simona, having finished her lunch, said: "Let's lie down for a sun-bath now."

"Will you be my pillow, Simona?" Livio asked, sliding toward her with the plain intention of putting his head on her lap.

For the first time Simona took her husband's presence into account.

"It's too hot for that, and you're too heavy."

And she looked at Giacomo out of the corner of her eyes as if to say: From now on, I won't let anyone do that but you. Giacomo's spirits soared, and he once more felt that there was a possibility of love between them. He got up and said: "Shall we go for a walk among the rocks?"

"Yes," she said promptly, following his example. And she added, to Livio: "See you later. . . . We're going to explore."

"Have a good time," Livio threw after them.

Simona led the way through the passage which her husband had shown her before. She made straight for the black beach, sat down at the foot of a rock and said: "Stretch out and put your head on my legs. . . . You'll be more comfortable that way."

Overcome by joy, Giacomo threw his arms around her and drew her to him. He gave her a kiss, and Simona returned it, blowing hard through her nose, almost as if she were suffering. When they had drawn apart, she repeated: "Stretch out, and we'll snatch a bit of sleep together."

She leaned her back against the rock, and Giacomo, his heart overflowing with love, lay down and put his head on her lap. He closed his eyes, and Simona began to stroke his face. With a hesitant and timid motion, she passed her hand over his cheeks, under his chin and up to the top of his head, where she ran her fingers through his hair. When Giacomo opened his eyes for a split second he saw that she was looking at him with childish intentness and curiosity. Meeting his glance, she bent over, placed a quick kiss on each of his eyes and told him to go to sleep. Giacomo closed his eyes again and gave himself up to enjoyment of the light touch of her tireless little hand until finally he dozed off. He slept for an indefinable length of time and woke up feeling chilled. Simona was sitting in the same position, with his head on her lap. Looking up, he saw the reason for his feeling so cold. The sky was filled with heavy, black storm clouds.

"How long have I been asleep?" he asked her.

"About an hour."

"And what about you?"

"I didn't sleep. I was looking at you."

"The sun's disappeared."

"Yes."

"There's going to be quite a rainstorm."

"Livio's gone," she said by way of an answer.

"Who is that Livio, anyhow?" Giacomo asked without moving.

"A Party comrade, a friend."

"I don't care for him."

"I know that," she said with a smile. "You made it pretty plain. As he was going away he pointed to you as you lay there asleep and said: 'What's the matter? Has he got it in for me?' "

"I haven't got it in for him. . . . But he has no manners. I'm on my honeymoon, and he acts as if it were his."

"He's a good fellow."

"You used to be in love with him. Admit it!"

She came out with a peal of innocent, silvery laughter.

"You must be crazy. I couldn't possibly fall in love with him. He doesn't appeal to me in the least."

"But the way you talked to one another . . ."

"He's a Party comrade," she repeated, "and that's the way we talk." She was silent, for a moment, and then said with unexpected bitterness: "He's unintelligent. That's why he doesn't appeal to me."

"He doesn't seem to me much more stupid than the next man."

"He said a lot of foolish things," she went on angrily. "That we'd kill people off, for instance. . . . He knows better and spoke that way just to show off. . . . But such loose talk is harmful to the Party."

"You're the one that's got it in for him now."

"No. I haven't got it in for him; but he had no business to talk that way." Then she added, more coolly, "As a matter of fact, he's of value to the Party, even if he isn't too bright. He's absolutely loyal; you could ask him to do anything."

"And what value have I?" Giacomo was bold enough to ask jokingly.

"You can't have any value, since you're not one of us."

Giacomo was displeased by this answer. He got up and looked at the lowering sky.

"We'd better get back home before it rains. What do you say?"

"Yes. I think we had better."

Giacomo hesitated for a moment, put his arm around her waist and asked softly: "When we get there, will you be mine . . . at last?"

She nodded, turning her head away in order not to meet his eyes. Feeling easier in his mind, Giacomo quickly got dressed. A few steps away, Simona pulled on her shorts and jersey and started to adjust her bag over her shoulder. But with a tender protectiveness such as he had not displayed on the way down, Giacomo said: "I'll carry that for you."

They started off. First they crossed the flatland, where the pale green branches of the prickly pears seemed to gleam discordantly against the dark sky. As they reached the beginning of the slope they turned around to look behind them. The pink-and-white lighthouse stood out against a majestic mass of black storm clouds rising from the horizon to invade that part of the sky which was still empty. These clouds, shaped like great rampant beasts, had smoking underbellies, and irregular fringes hung down from them over the sea, which was spottily darkening in some places, while in others it still shone like burnished lead in the sun. The fringes were gusts of rain, just beginning to comb the surface of the water. Meanwhile, a turbulent wind covered the prickly pears with yellow dust and a blinding stroke of lightning zigzagged diagonally across the sky from one point to another. After a long silence they heard the thunder—no clap, but rather a dull rumble within the clouds. Giacomo saw his wife pale and instinctively shrink toward him.

"Lightning scares me to death," she said, looking at him. Giacomo raised his eyes to the half-clear, half-stormy sky.

"The storm isn't here yet," he said. "It's still over the sea. If we hurry, we may get home without a wetting."

"Let's hurry, then," she said, continuing to climb up the path.

The clouds, apparently driven by an increasingly powerful wind, were spreading out over the sky with startling rapidity. Simona quickened her pace to almost a run, and Giacomo could not help teasing her.

"Afraid of lightning? What would the comrades say to that? A good Marxist like yourself shouldn't have any such fear."

"It's stronger than I am," she said in a childish voice, without turning around.

There were steps, first narrow and then wide, to facilitate the ascent of the lower part of the path, and higher up it rose in wide curves through groves of olive trees. Simona was a long way ahead; Giacomo could see her striding along fifty or sixty feet in front of him. At the top they paused to catch their breath and look around. Anacapri, momentarily at their backs, stood reassuringly behind a barrier of green, looking like an Arab city, with its terraces, campanile and gray-domed church. Giacomo pointed to the shrunken lighthouse on the promontory below, profiled against the threatening storm.

"Just think, we were right down there!" he murmured.

"I can't wait to be home," said Simona, perhaps with the thunder and lightning in mind. Then, meeting Giacomo's eyes, she added with hesitant coquetry: "What about you?"

"I agree," he answered in a low voice, with emotion.

The climb was over, and all they had to do now was follow

the level path to their rented house, which was well this side of Anacapri. They walked by the wall around the Munthe villa, along a meadow planted with oak trees, and there, just round a bend, was the white wall of their house and the rusty iron gate in the shade of a carob tree with pods hanging all over it. The clouds were straight above them now, and it was as dark as evening. Simona hurriedly pushed open the gate and went on ahead without waiting for her husband to follow. Giacomo walked more slowly down the marble steps among the cactus plants. As he went, there was another rumble of thunder, louder this time, like an overturned wagon-load of stones rolling down a hill. From inside the house Simona called back: "Shut the door tight!"

The house was on a hillside, set back among the trees, and consisted of four roughly furnished rooms. Giacomo made his way in amid almost complete darkness. There was no electric light, but oil lamps of various shapes and colors were lined up on the hall table. He lifted the glass off one of these, lit a match, touched it to the wick, put back the glass and entered the dining room. No one was there, but he could hear Simona moving in the room next to it. He did not wish to join her immediately, and, feeling thirsty, he poured himself out a glass of white wine. Finally, he picked up the lamp and went to the bedroom door. The bedroom, too, was almost dark. The window giving on to the garden was open, and through it, in what light was left among the shadows, he could make out the terrace surrounded by lemon trees planted in big pots. Simona, in a dressing gown, was tidying the still unmade bed. He set the lamp down on the bedside table and said: "Are you still afraid of the lightning?"

She was leaning over the bed, with one leg slightly raised, smoothing the sheet. Pulling herself up, she answered: "No. Now that I'm in the house I feel safer."

"And are you afraid of me?"

"I never was afraid of you."

Giacomo walked around the bed and took her into his arms. Standing beside the head of the bed, they exchanged a kiss. Giacomo undid the sash of Simona's dressing gown and it slipped down over her shoulders and hips to the floor. But Simona did not interrupt the kiss; indeed she prolonged it with an awkward eagerness, betrayed by her characteristic way of blowing through her nose. With sudden decisiveness, Giacomo let her go.

"Lie down, will you?" he said, hurriedly taking off his clothes.

Simona hesitated and then lay down on the bed. Giacomo was aware of being impelled by strictly animal feelings, as if he were not in a house, but in a dark cave—yes, as if he were a primitive man, moved by carnal appetite alone. Yet it was with a certain tenderness that he lay down beside his wife. She was facing the wall, but brusquely she turned around and pressed herself against him, snuggling into his arms. For a few minutes they lay there, motionless, then Giacomo began chastely and gently to caress her. He wanted to possess her on her own virginal terms, without bringing any of his masculine experience into play. His light caresses and the words he whispered through her hair into one ear were intended to calm her fears and lead her almost insensibly to give herself to him. He was not in a hurry and it seemed to him that his new policy of consideration and patience would win for him what his haste of the previous evening had failed to obtain. And by degrees he had the impression that, in response to his words and caresses, she was yielding not only her body, but also that inward part of her which had resisted him heretofore. Simona did not speak, but her breathing grew gradually heavier. All of a sudden, almost involuntarily, he gave way to a natural impulse and attempted to take her. Under the impact of his body, Simona seemed at first to surrender, then brusquely she rebelled and struggled to free herself. With a mixture of anger and submission she whispered: "I can't do it! I can't!"

Giacomo refused to heed her change of heart and tried to prevail over her by force. She defended herself with her feet and knees and hands, while he did everything to overcome her. In the combat their naked bodies were bathed in perspiration. Finally Giacomo lost his patience, leaped out of bed, and went into the bathroom, saying: "I'll be back in a minute."

Guided by a furious inspiration, he groped his way to the wash basin, took the razor blade he had used for shaving that morning and plunged it into the cushion of his thumb. He felt the cold blade cut through his skin, but had no pain. Then he put the blade back on the shelf and squeezed his thumb, which gave out an abundant flow of blood. He went back to the bedroom and threw himself upon his wife, rubbing his bloody thumb on the sheet between her legs. Then he shouted angrily: "You may not realize it, but you're no longer a virgin!"

Tremblingly she asked: "How do you know?"

"Just look!"

He took the lamp from the table and threw its light upon the bed. Simona was hunched up on the pillow, with her knees against her chin and her arms crossed over breasts. She looked down at the place where Giacomo had thrown the light and saw a long streak of red blood. Batting her eyelids in disgust, she said: "Are you sure?"

"Positive!"

But just at that moment her eyes traveled to the hand in which Giacomo was holding the lamp. Blood was streaming out of the cut in the cushion of his thumb. In a plaintive voice she cried out: "It's not my blood. It's yours! . . . You cut yourself on purpose."

Giacomo put the lamp back on the table and shouted in a rage: "That's the only blood I'll see tonight or any night to come. You're still a virgin and you always will be!"

"Why do you say that? What makes you so unkind?"

"That's the way it is," he answered. "You'll never be mine. Some part of you is hostile to me, and hostile it will remain."

"What part do you mean?"

"You're closer to that fool, Livio, than you are to me," he said, coming out with his jealousy at last. "That part of you which is close to Livio is hostile to me."

"That's not true."

"Yes; it is true. And it's equally true that if your Party came to power you'd inform on me. . . ."

"Who says so?"

"You said so yourself this morning, on the way to the light-house."

"I said nothing at all."

"Well, what would you do, then?"

She hesitated for a moment and then said:

"Why do you bring up such things at a time like this?"

"Because they prevent you from loving me and becoming my wife."

"I wouldn't inform on you," she said at last. "I'd leave you, that's all."

"But you're supposed to inform on your enemies," he shouted, angrier than ever. "It's your duty."

Still huddled up at the head of the bed, she burst into tears.

"Giacomo, why are you so unkind? . . . I'd kill myself. That's what I'd do."

Giacomo did not have the courage to remind her that on the way to the lighthouse she had branded suicide as morbid and absolutely inadmissible. After all, this contradiction was more flattering to him than an open declaration of love. Meanwhile, still in tears, she had got down from the bed and gone over to the open window. Giacomo lay on the bed, watching. She stood straight, with her head bent to the side and one arm raised against the frame. Suddenly the room was lit up, and every object in it, her naked, white body, the garden and the potted lemon trees around the terrace. There followed a metallic crack and a violent tremor which made the window and the walls of the room tremble. Simona gave a terrified cry, left the window and threw herself sobbing into her husband's arms. Giacomo pressed her to him, and almost immediately, while still weeping, she sought his embrace, he penetrated her body without any difficulty whatsoever. He had the feeling that a hidden flower, composed of only two petals, had opened—although still remaining invisible—to something that in the dark night of the flesh played the role of the sun. Nothing was settled, he reflected later on, but for the time being it was enough to know that she would kill herself for him.

Franz Kafka

THE METAMORPHOSIS

I

As Gregor Samsa awoke one morning from uneasy dreams he found himself transformed in his bed into a gigantic insect. He was lying on his hard, as it were armor-plated, back and when he lifted his head a little he could see his dome-like brown belly divided into stiff arched segments on top of which the bed quilt could hardly keep in position and was about to slide off completely. His numerous legs, which were pitifully thin compared to the rest of his bulk, waved helplessly before his eyes.

What has happened to me? he thought. It was no dream. His room, a regular human bedroom, only rather too small, lay quiet between the four familiar walls. Above the table on which a collection of cloth samples was unpacked and spread out—Samsa was a commercial traveler—hung the picture which he had recently cut out of an illustrated magazine and put into a pretty gilt frame. It showed a lady, with a fur cap on and a fur stole, sitting upright and holding out to the spectator a huge fur muff into which the whole of her forearm had vanished!

Gregor's eyes turned next to the window, and the overcast sky—one could hear rain drops beating on the window gutter—made him quite melancholy. What about sleeping a little longer and forgetting all this nonsense, he thought, but it could not be done, for he was accustomed to sleep on his right side and in his present condition he could not turn himself over. However violently he forced himself toward his right side he always rolled on to his back again. He tried it at least a hundred times, shutting his eyes to keep from seeing his struggling legs, and only desisted when

Translated by Willa and Edwin Muir. Reprinted by permission of Schocken Books Inc., from *The Penal Colony* by Franz Kafka. Copyright © 1948 by Schocken Books, Inc.

he began to feel in his side a faint dull ache he had never experienced before.

Oh God, he thought, what an exhausting job I've picked on! Traveling about day in, day out. It's much more irritating work than doing the actual business in the office, and on top of that there's the trouble of constant traveling, of worrying about train connections, the bed and irregular meals, casual acquaintances that are always new and never become intimate friends. The devil take it all! He felt a slight itching up on his belly; slowly pushed himself on his back nearer to the top of the bed so that he could lift his head more easily; identified the itching place which was surrounded by many small white spots the nature of which he could not understand and made to touch it with a leg, but drew the leg back immediately, for the contact made a cold shiver run through him.

He slid down again into his former position. This getting up early, he thought, makes one quite stupid. A man needs his sleep. Other commercials live like harem women. For instance, when I come back to the hotel of a morning to write up the orders I've got, these others are only sitting down to breakfast. Let me just try that with my chief; I'd be sacked on the spot. Anyhow, that might be quite a good thing for me, who can tell? If I didn't have to hold my hand because of my parents I'd have given notice long ago, I'd have gone to the chief and told him exactly what I think of him. That would knock him endways from his desk! It's a queer way of doing, too, this sitting on high at a desk and talking down to employees, especially when they have to come quite near because the chief is hard of hearing. Well, there's still hope; once I've saved enough money to pay back my parents' debts to him—that should take another five or six years—I'll do it without fail. I'll cut myself completely loose then. For the moment, though, I'd better get up, since my train goes at five.

He looked at the alarm clock ticking on the chest. Heavenly Father! he thought. It was half-past six o'clock and the hands were quietly moving on, it was even past the half-hour, it was getting on toward a quarter to seven. Had the alarm clock not gone off? From the bed one could see that it had been properly set for four o'clock; of course it must have gone off. Yes, but was it possible to sleep quietly through that ear-splitting noise? Well, he had not slept quietly, yet apparently all the more soundly for that. But what was he to do now? The next train went at seven o'clock; to catch that he would need to hurry like mad and his samples weren't even packed up, and he himself wasn't feeling particularly fresh and active. And even if he did catch the train he wouldn't avoid a row with the chief, since the firm's porter would have been waiting for the five o'clock train and would have long since reported his failure to turn up. The porter was a creature of the chief's, spineless and stupid. Well, supposing he were to say he was sick? But that would be most unpleasant and would look suspicious, since during his five years' employment he had not been ill once. The chief himself would be sure to come with the sick-insurance doctor, would reproach his parents with their son's laziness and would cut all excuses short by referring to the insurance doctor, who of course regarded all mankind as perfectly healthy malingerers. And would he be so far wrong on this occasion? Gregor really felt quite well, apart from a drowsiness that was utterly superfluous after such a long sleep, and he was even unusually hungry.

As all this was running through his mind at top speed without his being able to decide to leave his bed—the alarm clock had just struck a quarter to seven—there came a cautious tap at the door behind the head of his bed. "Gregor," said a voice—it was his mother's—"it's a quarter to seven. Hadn't you a train to catch?" That gentle voice! Gregor had a shock as he heard his own voice answering hers, unmistakably his own voice, it was true, but with a persistent horrible twittering squeak behind it like an undertone, that left the words in their clear shape only for the first moment and then rose up reverberating round them to destroy their sense, so that one could not be sure one had heard them rightly. Gregor wanted to answer at length and explain everything, but in the circumstances he confined himself to saying: "Yes, yes, thank you, Mother, I'm getting up now." The wooden door between them must have kept the change in his voice from being noticeable outside, for his mother contented herself with this statement and shuffled away. Yet this brief exchange of words had made the other members of the family aware that Gregor was still in the house, as they had not expected, and at one of the side doors his father was already knocking, gently, yet with his fist. "Gregor, Gregor," he called, "what's the matter with you?" And after a little while he called again in a deeper voice: "Gregor! Gregor!" At the other side door his sister was saying in a low, plaintive tone: "Gregor? Aren't you well? Are you needing anything?" He answered them both at once: "I'm just ready," and did his best to made his voice sound as normal as possible by enunciating the words very clearly and leaving long pauses between them. So his father went back to his breakfast, but his sister whispered: "Gregor, open the door, do." However, he was not thinking of opening the door, and felt thankful for the prudent habit he had acquired in traveling of locking all doors during the night, even at home.

His immediate intention was to get up quietly without being disturbed, to put on his clothes and above all eat his breakfast, and only then to consider what else was to be done, since in bed, he was well aware, his meditations would come to no sensible conclusion. He remembered that often enough in bed he had felt small aches and pains, probably caused by awkward postures, which had proved purely imaginary once he got up, and he looked forward eagerly to seeing this morning's delusions gradually fall away. That the change in his voice was nothing but the precursor of a severe chill, a standing ailment of commercial travelers, he had not the least possible doubt.

To get rid of the quilt was quite easy; he had only to inflate himself a little and it fell off by itself. But the next move was difficult, especially because he was so uncommonly broad. He would have needed arms and hands to hoist himself up; instead he had only the numerous little legs which never stopped waving in all directions and which he could not control in the least. When he tried to bend one of them it was the first to stretch itself straight; and did he succeed at last in making it do what he wanted, all the other legs meanwhile waved the more wildly in a high degree of unpleasant agitation. "But what's the use of lying idle in bed," said Gregor to himself.

He thought that he might get out of bed with the lower part of his body first, but this lower part, which he had not yet seen and of which he could form no clear conception, proved too difficult to move; it shifted so slowly; and when finally, almost wild with annoyance, he gathered his forces together and thrust out recklessly, he had miscalculated the direction and bumped heavily against the lower end of the bed, and the stinging pain he felt informed him that precisely this lower part of his body was at the moment probably the most sensitive.

So he tried to get the top part of himself out first, and cautiously moved his head towards the edge of the bed. That proved easy enough, and despite its breadth and mass the bulk of his body at last slowly followed the movement of his head. Still, when he finally got his head free over the edge of the bed he felt too scared to go on advancing, for after all if he let himself fall in this way it would take a miracle to keep his head from being injured. And at all costs he must not lose consciousness now, precisely now; he would rather stay in bed.

But when after a repetition of the same efforts he lay in his former position again, sighing, and watched his little legs struggling against each other more wildly than ever, if that were possible, and saw no way of bringing any order into this arbitrary confusion, he told himself again that it was impossible to stay in bed and that the most sensible course was to risk everything for the smallest hope of getting away from it. At the same time he did not forget meanwhile to remind himself that cool reflection, the coolest possible, was much better than desperate resolves. In such moments he focused his eyes as sharply as possible on the window, but, unfortunately, the prospect of the morning fog, which muffled even the other side of the narrow street, brought him little encouragement and comfort. "Seven o'clock already," he said to himself when the alarm clock chimed again, "seven o'clock already and still such a thick fog." And for a little while he lay quiet, breathing lightly, as if perhaps expecting such complete repose to restore all things to their real and normal condition.

But then he said to himself: "Before it strikes a quarter past seven I must be quite out of this bed, without fail. Anyhow, by that time someone will have come from the office to ask for me, since it opens before seven." And he set himself to rocking his whole body at once in a regular rhythm, with the idea of swinging it out of the bed. If he tipped himself out in that way he could keep his head from injury by lifting it at an acute angle when he fell. His back seemed to be hard and was not likely to suffer from a fall on the carpet. His biggest worry was the loud crash he would not be able to help making, which would probably cause anxiety, if not terror, behind all the doors. Still, he must take the risk.

When he was already half out of the bed—the new method was more a game than an effort, for he needed only to hitch himself across by rocking to and fro—it struck him how simple it would be if he could get help. Two strong people—he thought of his father and the servant girl—would be amply sufficient; they would only have to thrust their arms under his convex back, lever him out of the bed, bend down with their burden and then be patient enough to let him turn himself right over on to the floor, where it was to be hoped his legs would then find their proper function. Well, ignoring the fact that the doors were all locked, ought he really to call for help? In spite of his misery he could not suppress a smile at the very idea of it.

He had got so far that he could barely keep his equilibrium when he rocked himself strongly, and he would have to nerve himself very soon for the final decision since in five minutes' time it would be a quarter past seven—when the front door bell rang. "That's someone from the office," he said to himself, and grew almost rigid, while his little legs only jigged about all the faster. For a moment everything stayed quiet. "They're not going to open the door," said Gregor to himself, catching at some kind of irrational hope. But then of course the servant girl went as usual to the door with her heavy tread and opened it. Gregor needed only to hear the first good morning of the visitor to know immediately who it was—the chief clerk himself. What a fate, to be condemned to work for a firm where the smallest omission at once gave rise to the gravest suspicion! Were all employees in a body nothing but scoundrels, was there not among them one single loyal devoted man who, had he wasted only an hour or so of the firm's time in a morning, was so tormented by conscience as to be driven out of his mind and actually incapable of leaving his bed? Wouldn't it really have been sufficient to send an apprentice to inquire—if any inquiry were necessary at all—did the chief clerk himself have to come and thus indicate to the entire family, an innocent family, that this suspicious circumstance could be investigated by no one less versed in affairs than himself? And more through the agitation caused by these reflections than through any act of will Gregor swung himself out of bed with all his strength. There was a loud thump, but it was not really a crash. He fall was broken to some extent by the carpet, his back, too, was less stiff than he thought, and so there was merely a dull thud, not so very startling. Only he had not lifted his head carefully enough and had hit it; he turned it and rubbed it on the carpet in pain and irritation.

"That was something falling down in there," said the chief clerk in the next room to the left. Gregor tried to suppose to himself that something like what had happened to him today might some day happen to the chief clerk; one really could not deny that it was possible. But as if in brusque reply to this supposition the chief clerk took a couple of firm steps in the next-door room and his patent leather boots creaked. From the right-hand room his sister was whispering to inform him of the situation: "Gregor, the chief clerk's here." "I know," muttered Gregor to himself; but he didn't dare to make his voice loud enough for his sister to hear it.

"Gregor," said his father now from the left-hand room, "the chief clerk has come and wants to know why you didn't catch the early train. We don't know what to say to him. Besides, he wants to talk to you in person. So open the door, please. He will be good enough to excuse the untidiness of your room." "Good morning, Mr. Samsa," the chief clerk was calling amiably meanwhile. "He's not well," said his mother to the visitor, while his father was still speaking through the door, "he's not well, sir, believe me. What else would make him miss a train! The boy thinks about nothing but his work. It makes me almost cross the way he never goes out in the evenings; he's been here the last eight days and has stayed at home every single evening. He just sits there quietly at the table reading a newspaper or looking through railway timetables. The only amusement he gets is doing fretwork. For instance, he spent two or three evenings cutting out a little picture frame; you would be surprised to see how pretty it is; it's hanging in his room; you'll see it in a minute when Gregor opens the door. I must say I'm glad you've come, sir; we should never have got him to unlock the door by ourselves; he's so obstinate; and I'm sure he's unwell, though he wouldn't have it to be so this morning." "I'm just coming," said Gregor slowly and carefully, not moving an inch for fear of losing one word of the conversation. "I can't think of any other explanation, madam," said the chief clerk, "I hope it's nothing serious. Although on the other hand I must say that we men of business—fortunately or unfortunately—very often simply have to ignore any slight indisposition, since business must be attended to." "Well, can the chief clerk come in now?" asked Gregor's father impatiently, again knocking on the door. "No," said Gregor. In the left-hand room a painful silence followed this refusal, in the right-hand room his sister began to sob.

Why didn't his sister join the others? She was probably newly out of bed and hadn't even begun to put on her clothes yet. Well, why was she crying? Because he wouldn't get up and let the chief clerk in, because he was in danger of losing his job, and because the chief would begin dunning his parents again for the old debts? Surely these were things one didn't need to worry about for the present. Gregor was still at home and not in the least thinking of deserting the family. At the moment, true, he was lying on the carpet and no one who knew the condition he was in could seriously expect him to admit the chief clerk. But for such a small discourtesy, which could plausibly be explained away somehow later on, Gregor could hardly be dismissed on the spot. And it seemed to Gregor that it would be much more sensible to leave him in peace for the present than to trouble him with tears and entreaties. Still, of course, their uncertainty bewildered them all and excused their behavior.

"Mr. Samsa," the chief clerk called now in a louder voice, "what's the matter with you? Here you are, barricading yourself in your room, giving only 'yes' and 'no' for answers, causing your parents a lot of unnecessary trouble and neglecting—I mention this only in passing—neglecting your business duties in an incredible fashion. I am speaking here in the name of your parents and of your chief, and I beg you quite seriously to give me an immediate and precise explanation. You amaze me, you amaze me. I thought you were a quiet, dependable person, and now all at once you seem bent on making a disgraceful exhibition of yourself. The chief did hint to me early this morning a possible explanation for your disappearance—with reference to the cash payments that were entrusted to you recently—but I almost pledged my solemn word of honor that this could not be so. But now that I see how incredibly obstinate you are, I no longer have the slightest desire to take your part at all. And your position in the firm is not so unassailable. I came with the intention of telling you all this in private, but since you are wasting my time so needlessly I don't see why your parents shouldn't hear it too. For some time past your work has been most unsatisfactory; this is not the season of the year for a business boom, of course, we admit that, but a season of the year for doing no business at all, that does not exist, Mr. Samsa, must not exist."

"But, sir," cried Gregor, beside himself and in his agitation forgetting everything else, "I'm just going to open the door this very minute. A slight illness, an attack of giddiness, has kept me from getting up. I'm still lying in bed. But I feel all right again. I'm getting out of bed now. Just give me a moment or two longer! I'm not quite so well as I thought. But I'm all right really. How a thing like that can suddenly strike one down! Only last night I was quite well, my parents can tell you, or rather I did have a slight presentiment. I must have showed some sign of it. Why didn't I report it at the office! But one always thinks that an indisposition can be got over without staying in the house. Oh sir, do spare my parents! All that you're reproaching me with now has no foundation; no one has ever said a word to me about it. Perhaps you haven't looked at the last orders I sent in. Anyhow, I can still catch the eight o'clock train, I'm much the better for my few hours' rest. Don't let me detain you here, sir; I'll be attending to business very soon, and do be good enough to tell the chief so and to make my excuses to him!"

And while all this was tumbling out pell-mell and Gregor hardly knew what he was saying, he had reached the chest quite easily, perhaps because of the practice he had had in bed, and was now trying to lever himself upright by means of it. He meant actually to open the door, actually to show himself and speak to the chief clerk; he was eager to find out what the others, after all their insistence, would say at the sight of him. If they were horrified then the responsibility was no longer his and he could stay quiet. But if they took it calmly, then he had no reason either to be upset, and could really get to the station for the eight o'clock train if he hurried. At first he slipped down a few times from the polished surface of the chest, but at length with a last heave he stood upright; he paid no more attention to the pains in the lower part of his body, however they smarted. Then he let himself fall against the back of a nearby chair, and clung with his little legs to the edges of it. That brought him into control of himself again and he stopped speaking, for now he could listen to what the chief clerk was saying.

"Did you understand a word of it?" the chief clerk was asking; "surely he can't be trying to make fools of us?" "Oh dear," cried his mother, in tears, "perhaps he's terribly ill and we're tormenting him. Grete! Grete!" she called out then. "Yes Mother?" called his sister from the other side. They were calling to each other across

Gregor's room. "You must go this minute for the doctor. Gregor is ill. Go for the doctor, quick. Did you hear how he was speaking?" "That was no human voice," said the chief clerk in a voice noticeably low beside the shrillness of the mother's. "Anna! Anna!" his father was calling through the hall to the kitchen, clapping his hands, "get a locksmith at once!" And the two girls were already running through the hall with a swish of skirts—how could sister have got dressed so quickly?—and were tearing the front door open. There was no sound of its closing again; they had evidently left it open, as one does in houses where some great misfortune has happened.

But Gregor was now much calmer. The words he uttered were no longer understandable, apparently, although they seemed clear enough to him, even clearer than before, perhaps because his ear had grown accustomed to the sound of them. Yet at any rate people now believed that something was wrong with him, and were ready to help him. The positive certainty with which these first measures had been taken comforted him. He felt himself drawn once more into the human circle and hoped for great and remarkable results from both the doctor and the locksmith, without really distinguishing precisely between them. To make his voice as clear as possible for the decisive conversation that was now imminent he coughed a little, as quietly as he could, of course, since this noise too might not sound like a human cough for all he was able to judge. In the next room meanwhile there was complete silence. Perhaps his parents were sitting at the table with the chief clerk, whispering, perhaps they were all leaning against the door and listening.

Slowly Gregor pushed the chair toward the door, then let go of it, caught hold of the door for support—the soles at the end of his little legs were somewhat sticky—and rested against it for a moment after his efforts. Then he set himself to turning the key in the lock with his mouth. It seemed, unhappily, that he hadn't really any teeth—what could he grip the key with?—but on the other hand his jaws were certainly very strong; with their help he did manage to set the key in motion, heedless of the fact that he was undoubtedly damaging them somewhere, since a brown fluid issued from his mouth, flowed over the key and dripped on the floor. "Just listen to that," said the chief clerk next door; "he's turning the key." That was a great encouragement to Gregor; but they should all have shouted encouragement to him, his father and mother too: "Go on Gregor," they should have called out, "keep going, hold on to that key!" And in the belief that they were all following his efforts intently, he clenched his jaw recklessly on the key with all the force at his command. As the turning of the key progressed he circled round the lock, holding on now only with his mouth, pushing on the key, as required, or pulling it down again with all the weight of his body. The louder click of the finally yielding lock literally quickened Gregor. With a deep breath of relief he said to himself: "So I didn't need the locksmith," and laid his head on the handle to open the door wide.

Since he had to pull the door toward him, he was still invisible when it was really wide open. He had to edge himself slowly round the near half of the double door, and to do it very carefully if he was not to fall plump upon his back just on the threshold. He was still carrying out this difficult manoeuvre, with no time to observe anything else, when he heard the chief clerk utter a loud "Oh!"— it sounded like a gust of wind—and now he could see the man, standing as he was nearest to the door, clapping one hand before his open mouth and slowly backing away as if driven by some invisible steady pressure. His mother—in spite of the chief clerk's being there her hair was still undone and sticking up in all directions—first clasped her hands and looked at his father, then took two steps toward Gregor and fell on the floor among her outspread skirts, her face quite hidden on her breast. His father knotted his fist with a fierce expression on his face as if he meant to knock Gregor back into his room, then looked uncertainly round the living room, covered his eyes with his hands and wept till his great chest heaved.

Gregor did not go now into the living room, but leaned against the inside of the firmly shut wing of the door, so that only half his body was visible and his head above it bending sideways to look at the others. The light had meanwhile strengthened; on the other side of the street one could see clearly a section of the endlessly long, dark gray building opposite—it was a hospital– abruptly punctuated by its row of regular windows; the rain was still falling, but only in large singly discernible and literally singly splashing drops. The breakfast dishes were set out on the table lavishly, for breakfast was the most important meal of the day to Gregor's father, who lingered it out for hours over various newspapers. Right opposite Gregor on the wall hung a photograph of himself on military service, as a lieutenant, hand on sword, a carefree smile on his face, inviting one to respect his uniform and military bearing. The door leading to the hall was open, and one could see that the front door stood open too, showing the landing beyond and the beginning of the stairs going down.

"Well," said Gregor, knowing perfectly that he was the only one who had retained any composure, "I'll put my clothes on at once, pack up my samples and start off. Will you only let me go? You see, sir, I'm not obstinate, and I'm willing to work; traveling is a hard life, but I couldn't live without it. Where are you going, sir? To the office? Yes? Will you give a true account of all this? One can be temporarily incapacitated, but that's just the moment for remembering former services and bearing in mind that later on, when the incapacity has been got over, one will certainly work with all the more industry and concentration. I'm loyally bound to serve the chief, you know that very well. Besides, I have to provide for my parents and my sister. I'm in great difficulties, but I'll get out of them again. Don't make things any worse for me than they are. Stand up for me in the firm. Travelers are not popular there, I know. People think they earn sacks of money and just have a good time. A prejudice there's no particular reason for revising. But you, sir, have a more comprehensive view of affairs than the rest of the staff, yes, let me tell you in confidence, a more comprehensive view than the chief himself, who, being the owner, lets his judgment easily be swayed against one of his employees. And you know very well that the traveler, who is never seen in the office almost the whole year round, can so easily fall a victim to gossip and ill luck and unfounded complaints, which he mostly knows nothing about, except when he comes back exhausted from his rounds, and only then suffers in person from their evil consequences, which he can no longer trace back to the original causes. Sir, sir, don't go away without a word to me to show that you think me in the right at least to some extent!"

But at Gregor's very first words the chief clerk had already backed away and only stared at him with parted lips over one twitching shoulder. And while Gregor was speaking he did not stand still one moment but stole away towards the door, without taking his eyes off Gregor, yet only an inch at a time, as if obeying some secret injunction to leave the room. He was already at the hall, and the suddenness with which he took his last step out of the living room would have made one believe he had burned the sole of his foot. Once in the hall he stretched his right arm before him towards the staircase, as if some supernatural power were waiting there to deliver him.

Gregor perceived that the chief clerk must on no account be allowed to go away in this frame of mind if his position in the firm were not to be endangered to the utmost. His parents did not understand this so well; they had convinced themselves in the course of years that Gregor was settled for life in this firm, and besides they were so preoccupied with their immediate troubles that all foresight had forsaken them. Yet Gregor had this foresight. The chief clerk must be detained, soothed, persuaded and finally won over; the whole future of Gregor and his family depended on it! If only his sister had been there! She was intelligent; she had begun to cry while Gregor was still lying quietly on his back. And no doubt the chief clerk, so partial to ladies, would have been guided by her; she would have shut the door of the flat and in the hall talked him out of his horror. But she was not there, and Gregor would have to handle the situation himself. And without remembering that he was still unaware what powers of movement he possessed, without even remembering that his words in all possibility, indeed in all likelihood, would again be unintelligible, he let go the wing of the door, pushed himself through the opening, started to walk towards the chief clerk, who was already ridiculously clinging with both hands to the railing on the landing; but immediately, as he was feeling for a support, he fell down with a little cry upon all his numerous legs. Hardly was he down when he experienced for the first time this morning a sense of physical comfort; his legs had firm ground under them; they were completely obedient, as he noted with joy; they even strove to carry him forward in whatever direction he chose; and he was inclined to believe that a final relief from all his sufferings was at hand. But in the same moment as he found himself on the floor, rocking with suppressed eagerness to move, not far from his mother, indeed just in front of her, she, who had seemed so completely crushed, sprang all at once to her feet, her arms and fingers outspread, cried: "Help, for God's sake, help!" bent her head down as if to see Gregor better, yet on the contrary kept backing senselessly away; had quite forgotten that the laden table stood behind her; sat upon it hastily, as if in absence of mind, when she bumped into it; and seemed altogether unaware that the big coffee pot beside her was upset and pouring coffee in a flood over the carpet.

"Mother, Mother," said Gregor in a low voice, and looked up at her. The chief clerk, for the moment, had quite slipped from his mind; instead, he could not resist snapping his jaws together at the sight of the streaming coffee. That made his mother scream again, she fled from the table and fell into the arms of his father, who hastened to catch her. But Gregor had now no time to spare for his parents; the chief clerk was already on the stairs; with his chin on the banisters he was taking one last backward look. Gregor made a spring, to be as sure as possible of overtaking him; the chief clerk must have divined his intention, for he leaped down several steps and vanished; he was still yelling "Ugh!" and it echoed through the whole staircase.

Unfortunately, the flight of the chief clerk seemed completely to upset Gregor's father, who had remained relatively calm until now, for instead of running after the man himself, or at least not hindering Gregor in his pursuit, he seized in his right hand the walking stick which the chief clerk had left behind on a chair, together with a hat and greatcoat, snatched in his left hand a large newspaper from the table and began stamping his feet and flourishing the stick and the newspaper to drive Gregor back into his room. No entreaty of Gregor's availed, indeed no entreaty was even understood, however humbly he bent his head his father only stamped on the floor the more loudly. Behind his father his mother had torn open a window, despite the cold weather, and was leaning far out of it with her face in her hands. A strong draught set in from the street to the staircase, the window curtains blew in, the newspapers on the table fluttered, stray pages whisked over the floor. Pitilessly Gregor's father drove him back, hissing and crying "Shoo!" like a savage. But Gregor was quite unpracticed in walking backwards, it really was a slow business. If he only had a chance to turn round he could get back to his room at once, but he was afraid of exasperating his father by the slowness of such a rotation and at any moment the stick in his father's hand might hit him a fatal blow on the back or on the head. In the end, however, nothing else was left for him to do since to his horror he observed that in moving backwards he could not even control the direction he took; and so, keeping an anxious eye on his father all the time over his shoulder, he began to turn round as quickly as he could, which was in reality very slowly. Perhaps his father noted his good intentions, for he did not interfere except every now and then to help him in the manoeuvre from a distance with the point of the stick. If only he would have stopped making that unbearable hissing noise! It made Gregor quite lose his head. He had turned almost completely round when the hissing noice so distracted him that he even turned a little the wrong way again. But when at last his head was fortunately right in front of the doorway, it appeared that his body was too broad simply to get through the opening. His father, of course, in his present mood was far from thinking of such a thing as opening the other half of the door, to let Gregor have enough space. He had merely the fixed idea of driving Gregor back into his room as quickly as possible. He would never have suffered Gregor to make the circumstantial preparations for standing up on end and perhaps slipping his way through the door. Maybe he was now making more noise than ever to urge Gregor forward, as if no obstacle impeded him; to Gregor, any-how, the noise in his rear sounded no longer like the voice of one single father; this was really no joke, and Gregor thrust himself—come what might—into the doorway. One side of his body rose up, he was tilted at an angle in the doorway, his flank was quite bruised, horrid blotches stained the white door, soon he was stuck fast and, left to himself, could not have moved at all, his legs on one side fluttered trembling in the air, those on the other were crushed painfully to the floor—when from behind his father gave him a strong push which was literally a deliverance and he flew far into the room, bleeding freely. The door was slammed behind him with the stick, and then at last there was silence.

II

Not until it was twilight did Gregor awake out of a deep sleep, more like a swoon than a sleep. He would certainly have waked up of his own accord not much later, for he felt himself sufficiently rested and well-slept, but it seemed to him as if a fleeting step and a cautious shutting of the door leading into the hall had aroused him. The electric lights in the street cast a pale sheen here and there on the ceiling and the upper surfaces of the furniture, but down below, where he lay, it was dark. Slowly, awkwardly trying out his feelers, which he now first learned to appreciate, he pushed his way to the door to see what had been happening there. His left side felt like one single long, unpleasantly tense scar, and he had actually to limp on his two rows of legs. One little leg, moreover, had been severely damaged in the course of that morning's events—it was almost a miracle that only one had been damaged—and trailed uselessly behind him.

He had reached the door before he discovered what had really drawn him to it: the smell of food. For there stood a basin filled with fresh milk in which floated little sops of white bread. He could almost have laughed with joy, since he was now still hungrier than in the morning, and he dipped his head almost over the eyes straight into the milk. But soon in disappointment he withdrew it again; not only did he find it difficult to feed because of his tender left side—and he could only feed with the palpitating collaboration of his whole body—he did not like the milk either, although milk had been his favorite drink and that was certainly why his sister had set it there for him, indeed it was almost with repulsion that he turned away from the basin and crawled back to the middle of the room.

He could see through the crack of the door that the gas was turned on in the living room, but while usually at this time his father made a habit of reading the afternoon newspaper in a loud voice to his mother and occasionally to his sister as well, not a sound was now to be heard. Well, perhaps his father had recently given up this habit of reading aloud, which his sister had mentioned so often in conversation and in her letters. But there was the same silence all around, although the flat was certainly not empty of occupants. "What a quiet life our family has been leading," said Gregor to himself, and as he sat there motionless staring into the darkness he felt great pride in the fact that he had been able to provide such a life for his parents and sister in such a fine flat. But what if all the quiet, the comfort, the contentment were now to end in horror? To keep himself from being lost in such thoughts Gregor took refuge in movement and crawled up and down the room.

Once during the long evening one of the side doors was opened a little and quickly shut again, later the other side door too; someone had apparently wanted to come in and then thought better of it. Gregor now stationed himself immediately before the living room door, determined to persuade any hesitating visitor to come in or at least to discover who it might be; but the door was not opened again and he waited in vain. In the early morning, when the doors were locked, they had all wanted to come in, now that he had opened one door and the other had apparently been opened during the day, no one came in and even the keys were on the other side of the doors.

It was late at night before the gas went out in the living room, and Gregor could easily tell that his parents and his sister had all stayed awake until then, for he could clearly hear the three of them stealing away on tiptoe. No one was likely to visit him, not until the morning, that was certain; so he had plenty of time to meditate at his leisure on how he was to arrange his life afresh. But the lofty, empty room in which he had to lie flat on the floor filled him with an apprehension he could not account for, since it had been his very own room for the past five years—and with a half-unconscious action, not without a slight feeling of shame, he scuttled under the sofa, where he felt comfortable at once, although his back was a little cramped and he could not lift his head up, and his only regret was that his body was too broad to get the whole of it under the sofa.

He stayed there all night, spending the time partly in a light slumber, from which his hunger kept waking him up with a start, and partly in worrying and sketching vague hopes, which all led to the same conclusion, that he must lie low for the present and, by exercising patience and the utmost consideration, help the family to bear the inconvenience he was bound to cause them in his present condition.

Very early in the morning, it was still almost night, Gregor had the chance to test the strength of his new resolutions, for his sister, nearly fully dressed, opened the door from the hall and peered in. She did not see him at once, yet when she caught sight of him under the sofa—well, he had to be somewhere, he couldn't have flown away, could he?—she was so startled that without being able to help it she slammed the door shut again. But as if regretting her behavior she opened the door again immediately and came in on tiptoe, as if she were visiting an invalid or even a stranger. Gregor had pushed his head forward to the very edge of the sofa and watched her. Would she notice that he had left the milk standing, and not for lack of hunger, and would she bring in some other kind of food more to his taste? If she did not do it of her own accord, he would rather starve than draw her attention to the fact, although he felt a wild impulse to dart out from under the sofa, throw himself at her feet and beg her for something to eat. But his sister at once noticed, with surprise, that the basin was still full, except for a little milk that had been spilt all around it, she lifted it immediately, not with her bare hands, true, but with a cloth and carried it away. Gregor was wildly curious to know what she would bring instead, and made various speculations about it. Yet what she actually did next, in the goodness of her heart, he could never have guessed at. To find out what he liked she brought him a whole selection of food, all set out on an old newspaper. There were old, half-decayed vegetables, bones from last night's supper covered with a white sauce that had thickened; some raisins and almonds; a piece of cheese that Gregor would have called uneatable two days ago; a dry roll of bread, a buttered roll, and a roll both buttered and salted. Besides all that, she set down again the same basin, into which she had poured some water, and which was apparently to be reserved for his exclusive use. And with fine tact, knowing that Gregor would not eat in her presence, she withdrew quickly and even turned the key, to let him understand that he could take his ease as much as he liked. Gregor's legs all whizzed towards the food. He wounds must have healed completely, moreover, for he felt no disability, which amazed him and made him reflect how more than a month ago he had cut one finger a little with a knife and had still suffered pain from the wound only the day before yesterday. Am I less sensitive now? he thought, and sucked greedily at the cheese, which above all the other edibles attracted him at once and strongly. One after another and with tears of satisfaction in his eyes he quickly devoured the cheese, the vegetables and the sauce; the fresh food, on the other hand, had no charms for him, he could not even stand the smell of it and actually dragged away to some little distance the things he could eat. He had long finished his meal and was only lying lazily on the same spot when his sister turned the key slowly as a sign for him to retreat. That roused him at once, although he was nearly asleep, and he hurried under the sofa again. But it took considerable self-control for him to stay under the sofa, even for the short time his sister was in the room, since the large meal had swollen his body somewhat and he was so cramped he could hardly breathe. Slight attacks of breathlessness afflicted him and his eyes were starting a little out of his head as he watched his unsuspecting sister sweeping together with a broom not only the remains of what he had eaten but even the things he had not touched, as if these were now of no use to anyone, and hastily shoveling it all into a bucket, which she covered with a wooden lid and carried away. Hardly had she turned her back when Gregor came from under the sofa and stretched and puffed himself out.

In this manner Gregor was fed, once in the early morning while his parents and the servant girl were still asleep, and a second time after they had all had their midday dinner, for then his parents took a short nap and the servant girl could be sent out on some errand or other by his sister. Not that they would have wanted him to starve, of course, but perhaps they could not have borne to know more about his feeding than from hearsay, perhaps too his sister wanted to spare them such little anxieties wherever possible, since they had quite enough to bear as it was.

Under what pretext the doctor and the locksmith had been got rid of on that first morning Gregor could not discover, for since what he said was not understood by the others it never struck any of them, not even his sister, that he could understand what they said, and so whenever his sister came into his room he had to content himself with hearing her utter only a sigh now and then and an occasional appeal to the saints. Later on, when she had got a little used to the situation—of course she could never get completely used to it—she sometimes threw out a remark which was kindly meant or could be so interpreted. "Well, he liked his dinner today," she would say when Gregor had made a good clearance of his food; and when he had not eaten, which gradually happened more and more often, she would say almost sadly: "Everything's been left standing again."

But although Gregor could get no news directly, he overheard a lot from the neighboring rooms, and as soon as voices were audible, he would run to the door of the room concerned and press his whole body against it. In the first few days especially there was no conversation that did not refer to him somehow, even if only indirectly. For two whole days there were family consultations at every mealtime about what should be done; but also between meals the same subject was discussed, for there were always at least two members of the family at home, since no one wanted to be alone in the flat and to leave it quite empty was unthinkable. And on the very first of these days the household cook—it was not quite clear what and how much she knew of the situation—went down on her knees to his mother and begged leave to go, and when she departed, a quarter of an hour later, gave thanks for her dismissal with tears in her eyes as if for the greatest benefit that could have been conferred on her, and without any prompting swore a solemn oath that she would never say a single word to anyone about what had happened.

Now Gregor's sister had to cook too, helping her mother; true, the cooking did not amount to much, for they ate scarcely anything. Gregor was always hearing one of the family vainly urging another to eat and getting no answer but: "Thanks, I've had all I want," or something similar. Perhaps they drank nothing either. Time and again his sister kept asking his father if he wouldn't like some beer and offered kindly to go and fetch it herself, and when he made no answer suggested that she could ask the concierge to fetch it, so that he need feel no sense of obligation, but then a round "No" came from his father and no more was said about it.

In the course of that very first day Gregor's father explained the family's financial position and prospects to both his mother and his sister. Now and then he rose from the table to get some voucher or memorandum out of the small safe he had rescued from the collapse of his business five years earlier. One could hear him opening the complicated lock and rustling papers out and shutting it again. This statement made by his father was the first cheerful information Gregor had heard since his imprisonment. He had been of the opinion that nothing at all was left over from his father's business, at least his father had never said anything to the contrary, and of course he had not asked him directly. At that time Gregor's sole desire was to do his utmost to help the family to forget as soon as possible the catastrophe which had overwhelmed the business and thrown them all into a state of complete despair. And so he had set to work with unusual ardor and almost overnight had become a commercial traveler instead of a little clerk, with of course much greater chances of earning money, and his success was immediately translated into good round coin which he could lay on the table for his amazed and happy family. These had been fine times, and they had never recurred, at least not with the same sense of glory, although later on Gregor had earned so much money that he was able to meet the expenses of the whole household and did so. They had simply got used to it, both the family and Gregor; the money was gratefully accepted and gladly given, but there was no special uprush of warm feeling. With his sister alone had he remained intimate, and it was a secret plan of his that she, who loved music, unlike himself, and could play movingly on the violin, should be sent next year to study at the Conservatorium, despite the great expense that would entail, which must be made up in some other way. During his brief visits home the Conservatorium was often mentioned in the talks he had with his sister, but always merely as a beautiful dream which could never come true, and his parents discouraged even these innocent references to it; yet Gregor had made up his mind firmly about it and meant to announce the fact with due solemnity on Christmas Day.

Such were the thoughts, completely futile in his present condition, that went through his head as he stood clinging upright to the door and listening. Sometimes out of sheer weariness he had to give up listening and let his head fall negligently against the door, but he always had to pull himself together again at once, for even the slight sound his head made was audible next door and brought all conversation to a stop. "What can he be doing now?" his father would say after a while, obviously turning towards the door, and only then would the interrupted conversation gradually be set going again.

Gregor was now informed as amply as he could wish—for his father tended to repeat himself in his explanations, partly because it was a long time since he had handled such matters and partly because his mother could not always grasp things at once—that a certain amount of investments, a very small amount it was true, had survived the wreck of their fortunes and had even increased a little because the dividends had not been touched meanwhile. And besides that, the money Gregor brought home every month— he had kept only a few dollars for himself—had never been quite used up and now amounted to a small capital sum. Behind the door Gregor nodded his head eagerly, rejoiced at this evidence of unexpected thrift and foresight. True, he could really have paid off some more of his father's debts to the chief with this extra money, and so brought much nearer the day on which he could quit his job, but doubtless it was better the way his father had arranged it.

Yet this capital was by no means sufficient to let the family live on the interest of it; for one year, perhaps, or at the most two, they could live on the principal, that was all. It was simply a sum that ought not to be touched and should be kept for a rainy day; money for living expenses would have to be earned. Now his father was still hale enough but an old man, and he had done no work for the past five years and could not be expected to do much; during these five years, the first years of leisure in his laborious though unsuccessful life, he had grown rather fat and become sluggish. And Gregor's old mother, how was she to earn a living with her asthma, which troubled her even when she walked through the flat and kept her lying on a sofa every other day panting for breath beside an open window? And was his sister to earn her bread, she who was still a child of seventeen and whose life hitherto had been so pleasant, consisting as it did in dressing herself nicely, sleeping long, helping in the housekeeping, going out to a few modest entertainments and above all playing the violin? At first whenever the need for earning money was mentioned Gregor let go his hold on the door and threw himself down on the cool leather sofa beside it, he felt so hot with shame and grief.

Often he just lay there the long nights through without sleeping at all, scrabbling for hours on the leather. Or he nerved himself to the great effort of pushing an armchair to the window, then crawled up over the window sill and, braced against the chair, leaned against the window panes, obviously in some recollection of the sense of freedom that looking out of a window always used to give him. For in reality day by day things that were even a little way off were growing dimmer to his sight; the hospital across the street, which he used to execrate for being all too often before his eyes, was now quite beyond his range of vision, and if he had not known that he lived in Charlotte Street, a quiet street but still a city street, he might have believed that his window gave on a desert waste where gray sky and gray land blended indistinguishably into each other. His quick-witted sister only needed to observe twice that the armchair stood by the window; after that whenever she had tidied the room she always pushed the chair back to the same place at the window and even left the inner casements open.

If he could have spoken to her and thanked her for all she had to do for him, he could have borne her ministrations better; as it was, they oppressed him. She certainly tried to make as light as possible of whatever was disagreeable in her task, and as time went on she succeeded, of course, more and more, but time brought more enlightenment to Gregor too. The very way she came in distressed him. Hardly was she in the room when she rushed to the window, without even taking time to shut the door, careful as she was usually to shield the sight of Gregor's room from the others, and as if she were almost suffocating tore the casements open with hasty fingers, standing then in the open draught for a while even in the bitterest cold and drawing deep breaths. This noisy scurry of hers upset Gregor twice a day; he would crouch trembling under the sofa all the time, knowing quite well that she would certainly have spared him such a disturbance had she found it at all possible to stay in his presence without opening the window.

On one occasion, about a month after Gregor's metamorphosis, when there was surely no reason for her to be still startled at his appearance, she came a little earlier than usual and found him gazing out of the window, quite motionless, and thus well placed to look like a bogey. Gregor would not have been surprised had she not come in at all, for she could not immediately open the window while he was there, but not only did she retreat, she jumped back as if in alarm and banged the door shut; a stranger might well have thought that he had been lying in wait for her there meaning to bite her. Of course he hid himself under the sofa at once, but he had to wait until midday before she came again, and she seemed more ill at ease than usual. This made him realize how repulsive the sight of him still was to her, and that it was bound to go on being repulsive, and what an effort it must cost her not to run away even from the sight of the small portion of his body that stuck out from under the sofa. In order to spare her that, therefore, one day he carried a sheet on his back to the sofa— it cost him four hours' labor—and arranged it there in such a way as to hide him completely, so that even if she were to bend down she could not see him. Had she considered the sheet unnecessary, she would certainly have stripped it off the sofa again, for it was clear enough that this curtaining and confining of himself was not likely to conduce to Gregor's comfort, but she left it where it was, and Gregor even fancied that he caught a thankful glance from her eye when he lifted the sheet carefully a very little with his head to see how she was taking the new arrangement.

For the first fortnight his parents could not bring themselves to the point of entering his room, and he often heard them expressing their appreciation of his sister's activities, whereas formerly they had frequently scolded her for being as they thought a somewhat useless daughter. But now, both of them often waited outside the door, his father and his mother, while his sister tidied his room, and as soon as she came out she had to tell them exactly how things were in the room, what Gregor had eaten, how he had conducted himself this time and whether there was not perhaps some slight improvement in his condition. His mother, moreover, began relatively soon to want to visit him, but his father and sister dissuaded her at first with arguments which Gregor listened to very attentively and altogether approved. Later, however, she had to be held back by main force, and when she cried out: "Do let me in to Gregor, he is my unfortunate son! Can't you understand that I must go to him?" Gregor thought that it might be well to have her come in, not every day, of course, but perhaps once a week; she understood things, after all, much better than his sister, who was only a child despite the efforts she was making and had perhaps taken on so difficult a task merely out of childish thoughtlessness.

Gregor's desire to see his mother was soon fulfilled. During the daytime he did not want to show himself at the window, out of consideration for his parents, but he could not crawl very far around the few square yards of floor space he had, nor could he bear lying quietly at rest all during the night, while he was fast losing any interest he had ever taken in food, so that for mere recreation he had formed the habit of crawling crisscross over the walls and ceiling. He especially enjoyed hanging suspended from the ceiling; it was much better than lying on the floor; one could breathe more freely; one's body swung and rocked lightly; and in the almost blissful absorption induced by this suspension it could happen to his own surprise that he let go and fell plump on the floor. Yet he now had his body much better under control than formerly, and even such a big fall did him no harm. His sister at once remarked the new distraction Gregor had found for himself—he left traces behind him of the sticky stuff on his soles wherever he crawled—and she got the idea in her head of giving him as wide a field as possible to crawl in and of removing the pieces of furniture that hindered him, above all the chest of drawers and the writing desk. But that was more than she could manage all by herself; she did not dare ask her father to help her; and as for the servant girl, a young creature of sixteen who had had the courage to stay on after the cook's departure, she could not be asked to help, for she had begged as an especial favor that she might keep the kitchen door locked and open it only on a definite summons; so there was nothing left but to apply to her mother at an hour when her father was out. And the old lady did come, with exclamations of joyful eagerness, which, however, died away at the door of Gregor's room. Gregor's sister, of course, went in first, to see that everything was in order before letting his mother enter. In great haste Gregor pulled the sheet lower and rucked it more in folds so that it really looked as if it had been thrown accidentally over the sofa. And this time he did not peer out from under it; he renounced the pleasure of seeing his mother on this occasion and was only glad that she had come at all. "Come in, he's out of sight," said his sister, obviously leading her mother in by the hand. Gregor could now hear the two women struggling to shift the heavy old chest from its place, and his sister claiming the greater part of the labor for herself, without listening to the admonitions of her mother who feared she might overstrain herself. It took a long time. After at least a quarter of an hour's tugging his mother objected that the chest had better be left where it was, for in the first place it was too heavy and could never be got out before his father came home, and standing in the middle of the room like that it would only hamper Gregor's movements, while in the second place it was not at all certain that removing the furniture would be doing a service to Gregor. She was inclined to think to the contrary; the sight of the naked walls made her own heart heavy, and why shouldn't Gregor have the same feeling, considering that he had been used to his furniture for so long and might feel forlorn without it. "And doesn't it look," she concluded in a low voice—in fact she had been almost whispering all the time as if to avoid letting Gregor, whose exact whereabouts she did not know, hear even the tones of her voice, for she was convinced that he could not understand her words— "doesn't it look as if we were showing him, by taking away his furniture, that we have given up hope of his ever getting better and are just leaving him coldly to himself? I think it would be best to keep his room exactly as it has always been, so that when he comes back to us he will find everything unchanged and be able all the more easily to forget what has happened in between."

On hearing these words from his mother Gregor realized that the lack of all direct human speech for the past two months together with the monotony of family life must have confused his mind, otherwise he could not account for the fact that he had quite earnestly looked forward to having his room emptied of furnishing. Did he really want his warm room, so comfortably fitted with old family furniture, to be turned into a naked den in which he would certainly be able to crawl unhampered in all directions but at the price of shedding simultaneously all recollection of his human background? He had indeed been so near the brink of forgetfulness that only the voice of his mother, which he had not heard for so long, had drawn him back from it. Nothing should be taken out of his room; everything must stay as it was; he could not dispense with the good influence of the furniture on his state of mind; and even if the funiture did hamper him in his senseless crawling round and round, that was no drawback but a great advantage.

Unfortunately his sister was of the contrary opinion; she had grown accustomed, and not without reason, to consider herself an expert in Gregor's affairs as against her parents, and so her mother's advice was now enough to make her determined on the removal not only of the chest and the writing desk, which had been her first intention, but of all the furniture except the indispensable sofa. This determination was not, of course, merely the outcome of childish recalcitrance and of the self-confidence she had recently developed so unexpectedly and at such cost; she had in fact perceived that Gregor needed a lot of space to crawl about in, while on the other hand he never used the furniture at all, so far as could be seen. Another factor might have been also the enthusiastic temperament of an adolescent girl, which seeks to indulge itself on every opportunity and which now tempted Grete to exaggerate the horror of her brother's circumstances in order that she might do all the more for him. In a room where Gregor lorded it all alone over empty walls no one save herself was likely ever to set foot.

And so she was not to be moved from her resolve by her mother, who seemed moreover to be ill at ease in Gregor's room and therefore unsure of herself, was soon reduced to silence and helped her daughter as best she could to push the chest outside. Now, Gregor could do without the chest, if need be, but the writing desk he must retain. As soon as the two women had got the chest out of his room, groaning as they pushed it, Gregor stuck his head out from under the sofa to see how he might intervene as kindly and cautiously as possible. But as bad luck would have it, his mother was the first to return, leaving Grete clasping the chest in the room next door where she was trying to shift it all by herself, without of course moving it from the spot. His mother however was not accustomed to the sight of him, it might sicken her and so in alarm Gregor backed quickly to the other end of the sofa, yet could not prevent the sheet from swaying a little in front. That was enough to put her on the alert. She paused, stood still for a moment and then went back to Grete.

Although Gregor kept reassuring himself that nothing out of the way was happening, but only a few bits of furniture were being changed round, he soon had to admit that all this trotting to and fro of the two women, their little ejaculations and the scraping of furniture along the floor affected him like a vast disturbance coming from all sides at once, and however much he tucked in his head and legs and cowered to the very floor he was bound to confess that he would not be able to stand it for long. They were clearing his room out; taking away everything he loved; the chest in which he kept his fret saw and other tools was already dragged off; they were now loosening the writing desk which had almost sunk into the floor, the desk at which he had done all his homework when he was at the commercial academy, at the grammar school before that, and, yes, even at the primary school —he had no more time to waste in weighing the good intentions of the two women, whose existence he had by now almost forgotten, for they were so exhausted that they were laboring in silence and nothing could be heard but the heavy scuffling of their feet.

And so he rushed out—the women were just leaning against the writing desk in the next room to give themselves a breather— and four times changed his direction, since he really did not know what to rescue first, then on the wall opposite, which was already otherwise cleared, he was struck by the picture of the lady muffled in so much fur and quickly crawled up to it and pressed himself to the glass, which was a good surface to hold on to and comforted his hot belly. This picture at least, which was entirely hidden beneath him, was going to be removed by nobody. He turned his head toward the door of the living room so as to observe the women when they came back.

They had not allowed themselves much of a rest and were already coming; Grete had twined her arm round her mother and was almost supporting her. "Well, what shall we take now?" said Grete, looking round. Her eyes met Gregor's from the wall. She kept her composure, presumably because of her mother, bent her head down to her mother, to keep her from looking up, and said, although in a fluttering, unpremeditated voice: "Come, hadn't we better go back to the living room for a moment?" Her intentions were clear enough to Gregor, she wanted to bestow her mother in safety and then chase him down from the wall. Well, just let her try it! He clung to his picture and would not give it up. He would rather fly in Grete's face.

But Grete's words had succeeded in disquieting her mother, who took a step to one side, caught sight of the huge brown mass on the flowered wallpaper, and before she was really conscious that what she saw was Gregor screamed in a loud, hoarse voice: "Oh God, oh God!" fell with outspread arms over the sofa as if giving up and did not move. "Gregor!" cried his sister, shaking her fist and glaring at him. This was the first time she had directly addressed him since his metamorphosis. She ran into the next room for some aromatic essence with which to rouse her mother from her fainting fit. Gregor wanted to help too—there was still time to rescue the picture—but he was stuck fast to the glass and had to tear himself loose; he then ran after his sister into the next room as if he could advise her, as he used to do; but then had to stand helplessly behind her; she meanwhile searched among various small bottles and when she turned round started in alarm at the sight of him; one bottle fell on the floor and broke; a splinter of glass cut Gregor's face and some kind of corrosive medicine splashed him; without pausing a moment longer Grete gathered up all the bottles she could carry and ran to her mother with them; she banged the door shut with her foot. Gregor was now cut off from his mother, who was perhaps nearly dying because of him; he dared not open the door for fear of frightening away his sister, who had to stay with her mother; there was nothing he could do but wait; and harassed by self-reproach and worry he began now to crawl to and fro, over everything, walls, furniture and ceiling, and finally in his despair, when the whole room seemed to be reeling round him, fell down on to the middle of the big table.

A little while elapsed, Gregor was still lying there feebly and all around was quiet, perhaps that was a good omen. Then the doorbell rang. The servant girl was of course locked in her kitchen, and Grete would have to open the door. It was his father. "What's been happening?" were his first words; Grete's face must have told him everything. Grete answered in a muffled voice, apparently hiding her head on his breast: "Mother has been fainting, but she's better now. Gregor's broken loose." "Just what I expected," said his father, "just what I've been telling you, but you women would never listen." It was clear to Gregor that his father had taken the worst interpretation of Grete's all too brief statement and was assuming that Gregor had been guilty of some violent act. Therefore Gregor must now try to propitiate his father, since he had neither time nor means for an explanation. And so he fled to the door of his own room and crouched against it, to let his father see as soon as he came in from the hall that his son had the good intention of getting back into his room immediately and that it was not necessary to drive him there, but that if only the door were opened he would disappear at once.

Yet his father was not in the mood to perceive such fine distinctions. "Ah!" he cried as soon as he appeared, in a tone which sounded at once angry and exultant. Gregor drew his head back from the door and lifted it to look at his father. Truly, this was not the father he had imagined to himself; admittedly he had been too absorbed of late in his new recreation of crawling over the ceiling to take the same interest as before in what was happening elsewhere in the flat, and he ought really to be prepared for some changes. And yet, and yet, could that be his father? The man who used to lie wearily sunk in bed whenever Gregor set out on a business journey; who welcomed him back of an evening lying in a long chair in a dressing gown; who could not really rise to his feet but only lifted his arms in greeting, and on the rare occasions when he did go out with his family, on one or two Sundays a year and on high holidays, walked between Gregor and his mother, who were slow walkers anyhow, even more slowly than they did, muffled in his old greatcoat, shuffling laboriously forward with the help of his crook-handled stick which he set down most cautiously at every step and, whenever he wanted to say anything, nearly always came to a full stop and gathered his escort around him? Now he was standing there in fine shape; dressed in a smart blue uniform with gold buttons, such as bank messengers wear; his strong double chin bulged over the stiff high collar of his jacket; from under his bushy eyebrows his black eyes darted fresh and penetrating glances; his onetime tangled white hair had been combed flat on either side of a shining and carefully exact parting. He pitched his cap, which bore a gold monogram, probably the badge of some bank, in a wide sweep across the whole room on to a sofa and with the tail-ends of his jacket thrown back, his hands in his trouser pockets, advanced with a grim visage toward Gregor. Likely enough he did not himself know what he meant to do; at any rate he lifted his feet uncommonly high, and Gregor was dumbfounded at the enormous size of his shoe soles. But Gregor could not risk standing up to him, aware as he had been from the very first day of his new life that his father believed only the severest measures suitable for dealing with him. And so he ran before his father, stopping when he stopped and scuttling forward again when his father made any kind of move. In this way they circled the room several times without anything decisive happening, indeed the whole operation did not even look like a pursuit because it was carried out so slowly. And so Gregor did not leave the floor, for he feared that his father might take as a piece of peculiar wickedness any excursion of his over the walls or the ceiling. All the same, he could not stay this course much longer, for while his father took one step he had to carry out a whole series of movements. He was already beginning to feel breathless, just as in his former life his lungs had not been very dependable. As he was staggering along, trying to concentrate his energy on running, hardly keeping his eyes open; in his dazed state never even thinking of any other escape than simply going forward; and having almost forgotten that the walls were free to him, which in this room were well provided with finely carved pieces of furniture full of knobs and crevices—suddenly something lightly flung landed close behind him and rolled before him. It was an apple; a second apple followed immediately; Gregor came to a stop in alarm; there was no point in running on, for his father was determined to bombard him. He had filled his pockets with fruit from the dish on the sideboard and was now shying apple after apple, without taking particularly good aim for the moment. The small red apples rolled about the floor as if magnetized and cannoned into each other. An apple thrown without much force grazed Gregor's back and glanced off harmlessly. But another following immediately landed right on his back and sank in; Gregor wanted to drag himself forward, as if this startling, incredible pain could be left behind him; but he felt as if nailed to the spot and flattened himself out in a complete derangement of all his senses. With his last conscious look he saw the door of his room being torn open and his mother rushing out ahead of his screaming sister, in her underbodice, for her daughter had loosened her clothing to let her breathe more freely and recover from her swoon, he saw his mother rushing toward his father, leaving one after another behind her on the floor her loosened petticoats, stumbling over her petticoats straight to his father and embracing him, in complete union with him—but here Gregor's sight began to fail—with her hands clasped round his father's neck as she begged for her son's life.

III

The serious injury done to Gregor, which disabled him for more than a month—the apple went on sticking in his body as a visible reminder, since no one ventured to remove it—seemed to have made even his father recollect that Gregor was a member of the family, despite his present unfortunate and repulsive shape, and ought not to be treated as an enemy, that, on the contrary, family duty required the suppression of disgust and the exercise of patience, nothing but patience.

And although his injury had impaired, probably forever, his powers of movement, and for the time being it took him long, long minutes to creep across his room like an old invalid—there was no question now of crawling up the wall—yet in his own opinion he was sufficiently compensated for this worsening of his condition by the fact that towards evening the living-room door, which he used to watch intently for an hour or two beforehand, was always thrown open, so that lying in the darkness of his room, invisible to the family, he could see them all at the lamp-lit table and listen to their talk, by general consent as it were, very different from his earlier eavesdropping.

True, their intercourse lacked the lively character of former times, which he had always called to mind with a certain wistfulness in the small hotel bedrooms where he had been wont to throw himself down, tired out, on damp bedding. They were now mostly very silent. Soon after supper his father would fall asleep in his armchair; his mother and sister would admonish each other to be silent; his mother, bending low over the lamp, stitched at fine sewing for an underwear firm; his sister, who had taken a job as a salesgirl, was learning shorthand and French in the evenings on the chance of bettering herself. Sometimes his father woke up, and as if quite unaware that he had been sleeping said to his mother: "What a lot of sewing you're doing today!" and at once fell asleep again, while the two women exchanged a tired smile.

With a kind of mulishness his father persisted in keeping his uniform on even in the house; his dressing gown hung uselessly on its peg and he slept fully dressed where he sat, as if he were ready for service at any moment and even here only at the beck and call of his superior. As a result, his uniform, which was not brand-new to start with, began to look dirty, despite all the loving care of the mother and sister to keep it clean, and Gregor often spent whole evenings gazing at the many greasy spots on the garment, gleaming with gold buttons always in a high state of polish, in which the old man sat sleeping in extreme discomfort and yet quite peacefully.

As soon as the clock struck ten his mother tried to rouse his father with gentle words and to persuade him after that to get into bed, for sitting there he could not have a proper sleep and that was what he needed most, since he had to go on duty at six. But with the mulishness that had obsessed him since he became a bank messenger he always insisted on staying longer at the table, although he regularly fell asleep again and in the end only with the greatest trouble could be got out of his armchair and into his bed. However insistently Gregor's mother and sister kept urging him with gentle reminders, he would go on slowly shaking his head for a quarter of an hour, keeping his eyes shut, and refuse to get to his feet. The mother plucked at his sleeve, whispering endearments in his ear, the sister left her lessons to come to her mother's help, but Gregor's father was not to be caught. He would only sink down deeper in his chair. Not until the two women hoisted him up by the armpits did he open his eyes and look at them both, one after the other, usually with the remark: "This is a life. This is the peace and quiet of my old age." And leaning on the two of them he would heave himself up, with difficulty, as if he were a great burden to himself, suffer them to lead him as far as the door and then wave them off and go on alone, while the mother abandoned her needlework and the sister her pen in order to run after him and help him farther.

Who could find time, in this overworked and tried-out family, to bother about Gregor more than was absolutely needful? The household was reduced more and more; the servant girl was turned off; a gigantic bony charwoman with white hair flying round her head came in morning and evening to do the rough work; everything else was done by Gregor's mother, as well as great piles of sewing. Even various family ornaments, which his mother and sister used to wear with pride at parties and celebrations, had to be sold, as Gregor discovered of an evening from hearing them all discuss the prices obtained. But what they lamented most was the fact that they could not leave the flat which was much too big for their present circumstances, because they could not think of any way to shift Gregor. Yet Gregor saw well enough that consideration for him was not the main difficulty preventing the removal, for they could have easily shifted him in some suitable box with a few air holes in it; what really kept them from moving into another flat was rather their own complete hopelessness and the belief that they had been singled out for a misfortune such as had never happened to any of their relations or acquaintances. They fulfilled to the uttermost all that the world demands of poor people, the father fetched breakfast for the small clerks in the bank, the mother devoted her energy to making underwear for strangers, the sister trotted to and fro behind the counter at the behest of customers, but more than this they had not the strength to do. And the wound in Gregor's back began to nag at him afresh when his mother and sister, after getting his father into bed, came back again, left their work lying, drew close to each other and sat cheek by cheek; when his mother, pointing towards his room, said: "Shut that door now, Grete," and he was left again in darkness, while next door the women mingled their tears or perhaps sat dry-eyed staring at the table.

Gregor hardly slept at all by night or by day. He was often haunted by the idea that next time the door opened he would take the family's affairs in hand again just as he used to do; once more, after this long interval, there appeared in his thoughts the figures of the chief and the chief clerk, the commercial travelers and the apprentices, the porter who was so dull-witted, two or three friends in other firms, a chambermaid in one of the rural hotels, a sweet and fleeting memory, a cashier in a milliner's shop, whom he had wooed earnestly but too slowly—they all appeared, together with strangers or people he had quite forgotten, but instead of helping him and his family they were one and all unapproachable and he was glad when they vanished. At other times he would not be in the mood to bother about his family, he was only filled with rage at the way they were neglecting him, and although he had no clear idea of what he might care to eat he would make plans for getting into the larder to take the food that was after all his due, even if he were not hungry. His sister no longer took thought to bring him what might especially please him, but in the morning and at noon before she went to business hurriedly pushed into his room with her foot any food that was available, and in the evening cleared it out again with one sweep of the broom, heedless of whether it had been merely tasted, or—as most frequently happened—left untouched. The cleaning of his room, which she now did always in the evenings, could not have been more hastily done. Streaks of dirt stretched along the walls, here and there lay balls of dust and filth. At first Gregor used to station himself in some particularly filthy corner when his sister arrived, in order to reproach her with it, so to speak. But he could have sat there for weeks without getting her to make any improvement; she could see the dirt as well as he did, but she had simply made up her mind to leave it alone. And yet, with a touchiness that was new to her, which seemed anyhow to have infected the whole family, she jealously guarded her claim to be the sole caretaker of Gregor's room. His mother once subjected his room to a thorough cleaning, which was achieved only by means of several buckets of water—all this dampness of course upset Gregor too and he lay widespread, sulky and motionless on the sofa—but she was well punished for it. Hardly had his siter noticed the changed aspect of his room that evening than she rushed in high dudgeon into the living room and, despite the imploringly raised hands of her mother, burst into a storm of weeping, while her parents—her father had of course been startled out of his chair—looked on at first in helpless amazement; then they too began to go into action; the father reproached the mother on his right for not having left the cleaning of Gregor's room to his sister; shrieked at the sister on his left that never again was she to be allowed to clean Gregor's room; while the mother tried to pull the father into his bedroom, since he was beyond himself with agitation; the sister, shaken with sobs, then beat upon the table with her small fists; and Gregor hissed loudly with rage because not one of them thought of shutting the door to spare him such a spectacle and so much noise.

Still, even if the sister, exhausted by her daily work, had grown tired of looking after Gregor as she did formerly, there was no need for his mother's intervention or for Gregor's being neglected at all. The charwoman was there. This old widow, whose strong bony frame had enabled her to survive the worst a long life could offer, by no means recoiled from Gregor. Without being in the least curious she had once by chance opened the door of his room and at the sight of Gregor, who, taken by surprise, began to rush to and fro although no one was chasing him, merely stood there with her arms folded. From that time she never failed to open his door a little for a moment, morning and evening, to have a look at him. At first she even used to call him to her, with words which apparently she took to be friendly, such as: "Come along, then, you old dung beetle!" or "Look at the old dung beetle, then!" To such allocutions Gregor made no answer, but stayed motionless where he was, as if the door had never been opened. Instead of being allowed to disturb him so senselessly whenever the whim took her, she should rather have been ordered to clean out his room daily, that charwoman! Once, early in the morning—heavy rain was lashing on the windowpanes, perhaps a sign that spring was on the way—Gregor was so exasperated when she began addressing him again that he ran at her, as if to attack her, although slowly and feebly enough. But the charwoman instead of showing fright merely lifted high a chair that happened to be beside the door, and as she stood there with her mouth wide open it was clear that she meant to shut it only when she brought the chair down on Gregor's back. "So you're not coming any nearer?" she asked, as Gregor turned away again, and quietly put the chair back into the corner.

Gregor was now eating hardly anything. Only when he happened to pass the food laid out for him did he take a bit of something in his mouth as a pastime, kept it there for an hour at a time and usually spat it out again. At first he thought it was chagrin over the state of his room that prevented him from eating, yet he soon got used to the various changes in his room. It had become a habit in the family to push into his room things there was no room for elsewhere, and there were plenty of these now, since one of the rooms had been let to three lodgers. These serious gentlemen—all three of them with full beards, as Gregor once observed through a crack in the door—had a passion for order, not only in their own room but, since they were now members of the household, in all its arrangements, especially in the kitchen. Superfluous, not to say dirty, objects they could not bear. Besides, they had brought with them most of the furnishings they needed. For this reason many things could be dispensed with that it was no use trying to sell but that should not be thrown away either. All of them found their way into Gregor's room. The ash can likewise and the kitchen garbage can. Anything that was not needed for the moment was simply flung into Gregor's room by the charwoman, who did everything in a hurry; fortunately Gregor usually saw only the object, whatever it was, and the hand that held it. Perhaps she intended to take the things away again as time and opportunity offered, or to collect them until she could throw them all out in a heap, but in fact they just lay wherever she happened to throw them, except when Gregor pushed his way through the junk heap and shifted it somewhat, at first out of necessity, because he had not room enough to crawl, but later with increasing enjoyment, although after such excursions, being sad and weary to death, he would lie motionless for hours. And since the lodgers often ate their supper at home in the common living room, the living-room door stayed shut many an evening, yet Gregor reconciled himself quite easily to the shutting of the door, for often enough on evenings when it was opened he had disregarded it entirely and lain in the darkest corner of his room, quite unnoticed by the family. But on one occasion the charwoman left the door open a little and it stayed ajar even when the lodgers came in for supper and the lamp was lit. They set themselves at the top end of the table where formerly Gregor and his father and mother had eaten their meals, unfolded their napkins and took knife and fork in hand. At once his mother appeared in the other doorway with a dish of meat and close behind her his sister with a dish of potatoes piled high. The food steamed with a thick vapor. The lodgers bent over the food set before them as if to scrutinize it before eating, in fact the man in the middle, who seemed to pass for an authority with the other two, cut a piece of meat as it lay on the dish, obviously to discover if it were tender or should be sent back to the kitchen. He showed satisfaction, and Gregor's mother and sister, who had been watching anxiously, breathed freely and began to smile.

The family itself took its meals in the kitchen. None the less, Gregor's father came into the living room before going into the kitchen and with one prolonged bow, cap in hand, made a round of the table. The lodgers all stood up and murmured something in their beards. When they were alone again they ate their food in almost complete silence. It seemed remarkable to Gregor that among the various noises coming from the table he could always distinguish the sound of their masticating teeth, as if this were a sign to Gregor that one needed teeth in order to eat, and that with toothless jaws even of the finest make one could do nothing. "I'm hungry enough," said Gregor sadly to himself, "but not for that kind of food. How these lodgers are stuffing themselves, and here am I dying of starvation!"

On that very evening—during the whole of his time there Gregor could not remember ever having heard the violin—the sound of violin-playing came from the kitchen. The lodgers had already finished their supper, the one in the middle had brought out a newspaper and given the other two a page apiece, and now they were leaning back at ease reading and smoking. When the violin began to play they pricked up their ears, got to their feet, and went on tiptoe to the hall door where they stood huddled together. Their movements must have been heard in the kitchen, for Gregor's father called out: "Is the violin-playing disturbing you, gentlemen? It can be stopped at once." "On the contrary," said the middle lodger, "could not Fräulein Samsa come and play in this room, beside us, where it is much more convenient and comfortable?" "Oh certainly," cried Gregor's father, as if he were the violin-player. The lodgers came back into the living room and waited. Presently Gregor's father arrived with the music stand, his mother carrying the music and his sister with the violin. His sister quietly made everything ready to start playing; his parents, who had never let rooms before and so had an exaggerated idea of the courtesy due to lodgers, did not venture to sit down on their own chairs; his father leaned against the door, the right hand thrust between two buttons of his livery coat, which was formally buttoned up; but his mother was offered a chair by one of the lodgers and, since she left the chair just where he had happened to put it, sat down in a corner to one side.

Gregor's sister began to play; the father and mother, from either side, intently watched the movements of her hands. Gregor, attracted by the playing, ventured to move forward a little until his head was actually inside the living room. He felt hardly any surprise at his growing lack of consideration for the others; there had been a time when he prided himself on being considerate. And yet just on this occasion he had more reason than ever to hide himself, since owing to the amount of dust which lay thick in his room and rose into the air at the slightest movement, he too was covered with dust; fluff and hair and remnants of food trailed with him, caught on his back and along his sides; his indifference to everything was much too great for him to turn on his back and scrape himself clean on the carpet, as once he had done several times a day. And in spite of his condition, no shame deterred him from advancing a little over the spotless floor of the living room.

To be sure, no one was aware of him. The family was entirely absorbed in the violin-playing; the lodgers, however, who first of all had stationed themselves, hands in pockets, much too close behind the music stand so that they could all have read the music, which must have bothered his sister, had soon retreated to the window, half-whispering with downbent heads, and stayed there while his father turned an axious eye on them. Indeed, they were making it more than obvious thay they had been disappointed in their expectation of hearing good or enjoyable violin-playing, that they had had more than enough of the performance and only out of courtesy suffered a continued disturbance of their peace. From the way they all kept blowing the smoke of their cigars high in the air through nose and mouth one could divine their irritation. And yet Gregor's sister was playing so beautifully. Her face leaned sideways, intently and sadly her eyes followed the notes of music. Gregor crawled a little farther forward and lowered his head to the ground so that it might be possible for his eyes to meet hers. Was he an animal, that music had such an effect upon him? He felt as if the way were opening before him to the unknown nourishment he craved. He was determined to push forward till he reached his sister, to pull at her skirt and so let her know that she was to come into his room with her violin, for no one here appreciated her playing as he would appreciate it. He would never let her out of his room, at least, not so long as he lived; his frightful appearance would become, for the first time, useful to him; he would watch all the doors of his room at once and spit at intruders; but his sister should need no constraint, she should stay with him of her own free will; she should sit beside him on the sofa, bend down her ear to him and hear him confide that he had had the firm intention of sending her to the Conservatorium, and that, but for his mishap, last Christmas—surely Christmas was long past?—he would have announced it to everybody without allowing a single objection. After this confession his sister would be so touched that she would burst into tears, and Gregor would then raise himself to her shoulder and kiss her on the neck, which, now that she went to business, she kept free of any ribbon or collar.

"Mr. Samsa!" cried the middle lodger, to Gregor's father, and pointed, without wasting any more words, at Gregor, now working himself slowly forwards. The violin fell silent, the middle lodger first smiled to his friends with a shake of the head and then looked at Gregor again. Instead of driving Gregor out, his father seemed to think it more needful to begin by soothing down the lodgers, although they were not at all agitated and apparently found Gregor more entertaining than the violin-playing. He hurried towards them and, spreading out his arms, tried to urge them back into their own room and at the same time to block their view of Gregor. They now began to be really a little angry, one could not tell whether because of the old man's behavior or because it had just dawned on them that all unwittingly they had such a neighbor as Gregor next door. They demanded explanations of his father, they waved their arms like him, tugged uneasily at their beards, and only with reluctance backed towards their room. Meanwhile Gregor's sister, who stood there as if lost when her playing was so abruptly broken off, came to life again, pulled herself together all at once after standing for a while holding violin and bow in nervelessly hanging hands and staring at her music, pushed her violin into the lap of her mother, who was still sitting in her chair fighting asthmatically for breath, and ran into the lodgers' room to which they were now being shepherded by her father rather more quickly than before. One could see the pillows and blankets on the beds flying under her accustomed fingers and being laid in order. Before the lodgers had actually reached their room she had finished making the beds and slipped out.

The old man seemed once more to be so possessed by his mulish self-assertiveness that he was forgetting all the respect he should show to his lodgers. He kept driving them on and driving them on until in the very door of the bedroom the middle lodger stamped his foot loudly on the floor and so brought him to a halt. "I beg to announce," said the lodger, lifting one hand and looking also at Gregor's mother and sister, "that because of the disgusting conditions prevailing in this household and family"—here he spat on the door with emphatic brevity—"I give you notice on the spot. Naturally I won't pay you a penny for the days I have lived here, on the contrary I shall consider bringing an action for damages against you, based on claims—believe me—that will be easily susceptible of proof." He ceased and stared straight in front of him, as if he expected something. In fact his two friends at once rushed into the breach with these words: "And we too give notice on the spot." On that he seized the door-handle and shut the door with a slam.

Gregor's father, groping with his hands, staggered forward and fell into his chair; it looked as if he were stretching himself there for his ordinary evening nap, but the marked jerkings of his head, which was as if uncontrollable, showed that he was far from asleep. Gregor had simply stayed quietly all the time on the spot where the lodgers had espied him. Disappointment at the failure of his plan, perhaps also the weakness arising from extreme hunger, made it impossible for him to move. He feared, with a fair degree of certainty, that at any moment the general tension would discharge itself in a combined attack upon him, and he lay waiting. He did not react even to the noise made by the violin as it fell off his mother's lap from under her trembling fingers and gave out a resonant note.

"My dear parents," said his sister, slapping her hand on the table by way of introduction, "things can't go on like this. Perhaps you don't realize that, but I do. I won't utter my brother's name in the presence of this creature, and so all I say is: we must try to get rid of it. We've tried to look after it and to put up with it as far as is humanly possible, and I don't think anyone could reproach us in the slightest."

"She is more than right," said Gregor's father to himself. His mother, who was still choking for lack of breath, began to cough hollowly into her hand with a wild look in her eyes.

His sister rushed over to her and held her forehead. His father's thoughts seemed to have lost their vagueness at Grete's words, he sat more upright, fingering his service cap that lay among the plates still lying on the table from the lodgers' supper, and from time to time looked at the still form of Gregor.

"We must try to get rid of it," his sister now said explicitly to her father, since her mother was coughing too much to hear a word, "it will be the death of both of you, I can see that coming. When one has to work as hard as we do, all of us, one can't stand this continual torment at home on top of it. At least I can't stand it any longer." And she burst into such a passion of sobbing that her tears dropped on her mother's face, where she wiped them off mechanically.

"My dear," said the old man sympathetically, and with evident understanding, "but what can we do?"

Gregor's sister merely shrugged her shoulders to indicate the feeling of helplessness that had now overmastered her during her weeping fit, in contrast to her former confidence.

"If he could understand us," said her father, half questioningly; Grete, still sobbing, vehemently waved a hand to show how unthinkable that was.

"If he could understand us," repeated the old man, shutting his eyes to consider his daughter's conviction that understanding was impossible, "then perhaps we might come to some agreement with him. But as it is—"

"He must go," cried Gregor's sister, "that's the only solution, Father. You must just try to get rid of the idea that this is Gregor. The fact that we've believed it for so long is the root of all our trouble. But how can it be Gregor? If this were Gregor, he would have realized long ago that human beings can't live with such a creature, and he'd have gone away on his own accord. Then we wouldn't have any brother, but we'd be able to go on living and keep his memory in honor. As it is, this creature persecutes us, drives away our lodgers, obviously wants the whole apartment to himself and would have us all sleep in the gutter. Just look, Father," she shrieked all at once, "he's at it again!" And in an access of panic that was quite incomprehensible to Gregor she even quitted her mother, literally thrusting the chair from her as if she would rather sacrifice her mother than stay so near to Gregor, and rushed behind her father, who also rose up, being simply upset by her agitation, and half-spread his arms out as if to protect her.

Yet Gregor had not the slightest intention of frightening anyone, far less his sister. He had only begun to turn round in order to crawl back to his room, but it was certainly a startling operation to watch, since because of his disabled condition he could not execute the difficult turning movements except by lifting his head and then bracing it against the floor over and over again. He paused and looked round. His good intentions seemed to have been recognized; the alarm had only been momentary. Now they were all watching him in melancholy silence. His mother lay in her chair, her legs stiffly outstretched and pressed together, her eyes almost closing for sheer weariness; his father and his sister were sitting beside each other, his sister's arm around the old man's neck.

Perhaps I can go on turning round now, thought Gregor, and began his labors again. He could not stop himself from panting with the effort, and had to pause now and then to take breath. Nor did anyone harass him, he was left entirely to himself. When he had completed the turn-round he began at once to crawl straight back. He was amazed at the distance separating him from his room and could not understand how in his weak state he had managed to accomplish the same journey so recently, almost without remarking it. Intent on crawling as fast as possible, he barely noticed that not a single word, not an ejaculation from his family, interfered with his progress. Only when he was already in the doorway did he turn his head round, not completely, for his neck muscles were getting stiff, but enough to see that nothing had changed behind him except that his sister had risen to her feet. His last glance fell on his mother, who was not quite overcome by sleep.

Hardly was he well inside his room when the door was hastily pushed shut, bolted and locked. The sudden noise in his rear startled him so much that his little legs gave beneath him. It was his sister who had shown such haste. She had been standing ready waiting and had made a light spring forward, Gregor had not even heard her coming, and she cried "At last!" to her parents as she turned the key in the lock.

"And what now?" said Gregor to himself, looking round in the darkness. Soon he made the discovery that he was now unable to stir a limb. This did not surprise him, rather it seemed unnatural that he should ever actually have been able to move on these feeble little legs. Otherwise he felt relatively comfortable. True, his whole body was aching, but it seemed that the pain was gradually growing less and would finally pass away. The rotting apple in his back and the inflamed area around it, all covered with soft dust, already hardly troubled him. He thought of his family with tenderness and love. The decision that he must disappear was one that he held to even more strongly than his sister, if that were possible. In this state of vacant and peaceful meditation he remained until the tower clock struck three in the morning. The first broadening of light in the world outside the window entered his consciousness once more. Then his head sank to the floor of its own accord and from his nostrils came the last faint flicker of his breath.

When the charwoman arrived early in the morning—what between her strength and her impatience she slammed all the doors so loudly, never mind how often she had been begged not to do so, that no one in the whole apartment could enjoy any quiet sleep after her arrival—she noticed nothing unusual as she took her customary peep into Gregor's room. She thought he was lying motionless on purpose, pretending to be in the sulks; she credited him with every kind of intelligence. Since she happened to have the long-handled broom in her hand she tried to tickle him up with it from the doorway. When that too produced no reaction she felt provoked and poked at him a little harder, and only when she had pushed him along the floor without meeting any resistance was her attention aroused. It did not take her long to establish the truth of the matter, and her eyes widened, she let out a whistle, yet did not waste much time over it but tore open the door of the Samsas' bedroom and yelled into the darkness at the top of her voice: "Just look at this, it's dead; it's lying here dead and done for!"

Mr. and Mrs. Samsa started up in their double bed and before they realized the nature of the charwoman's announcement had some difficulty in overcoming the shock of it. But then they got out of bed quickly, one on either side, Mr. Samsa throwing a blanket over his shoulders, Mrs. Samsa in nothing but her nightgown; in this array they entered Gregor's room. Meanwhile the door of the living room opened, too, where Grete had been sleeping since the advent of the lodgers; she was completely dressed as if she had not been to bed, which seemed to be confirmed also by the paleness of her face. "Dead?" said Mrs. Samsa, looking questioningly at the charwoman, although she could have investigated for herself, and the fact was obvious enough without investigation. "I should say so," said the charwoman, proving her words by pushing Gregor's corpse a long way to one side with her broomstick. Mrs. Samsa made a movement as if to stop her, but checked it. "Well," said Mr. Samsa, "now thanks be to God." He crossed himself, and the three women followed his example. Grete, whose eyes never left the corpse, said: "Just see how thin he was. It's such a long time since he's eaten anything. The food came out again just as it went in." Indeed, Gregor's body was completely flat and dry, as could only now be seen when it was no longer supported by the legs and nothing prevented one from looking closely at it.

"Come in beside us, Grete, for a little while," said Mrs. Samsa with a tremulous smile, and Grete, not without looking back at the corpse, followed her parents into their bedroom. The charwoman shut the door and opened the window wide. Although it was so early in the morning a certain softness was perceptible in the fresh air. After all, it was already the end of March.

The three lodgers emerged from their room and were surprised to see no breakfast; they had been forgotten. "Where's our breakfast?" said the middle lodger peevishly to the charwoman. But she put her finger to her lips and hastily, without a word, indicated by gestures that they should go into Gregor's room. They did so and stood, their hands in the pockets of their somewhat shabby coats, around Gregor's corpse in the room where it now now fully light.

At that the door of the Samsas' bedroom opened and Mr. Samsa appeared in his uniform, his wife on one arm, his daughter on the other. They all looked a little as if they had been crying; from time to time Grete hid her face on her father's arm.

"Leave my house at once!" said Mr. Samsa, and pointed to the door without disengaging himself from the women. "What do you mean by that?" said the middle lodger, taken somewhat aback, with a feeble smile. The two others put their hands behind them and kept rubbing them together, as if in gleeful expectation of a fine set-to in which they were bound to come off the winners. "I mean just what I say," answered Mr. Samsa, and advanced in a straight line with his two companions towards the lodger. He stood his ground at first quietly, looking at the floor as if his thoughts were taking a new pattern in his head. "Then let us go, by all means," he said, and looked up at Mr. Samsa as if in a sudden access of humility he were expecting some renewed sanction for this decision. Mr. Samsa merely nodded briefly once or twice with meaning eyes. Upon that the lodger really did go with long strides into the hall, his two friends had been listening and had quite stopped rubbing their hands for some moments and now went scuttling after him as if afraid that Mr. Samsa might get into the hall before them and cut them off from their leader. In the hall they all three took their hats from the rack, their sticks from the umbrella stand, bowed in silence and quitted the apartment. With a suspiciousness which proved quite unfounded Mr. Samsa and the two women followed them out to the landing; leaning over the banister they watched the three figures slowly but surely going down the long stairs, vanishing from sight at a certain turn of the staircase on every floor and coming into view again after a moment or so; the more they dwindled, the more the Samsa family's interest in them dwindled, and when a butcher's boy met them and passed them on the stairs coming up proudly with a tray on his head, Mr. Samsa and the two women soon left the landing and as if a burden had been lifted from them went back into their apartment.

They decided to spend this day in resting and going for a stroll; they had not only deserved such a respite from work, but absolutely needed it. And so they sat down at the table and wrote three notes of excuse, Mr. Samsa to his board of management, Mrs. Samsa to her employer and Grete to the head of her firm. While they were writing, the charwoman came in to say that she was going now, since her morning's work was finished. At first they only nodded without looking up, but as she kept hovering there they eyed her irritably. "Well?" said Mr. Samsa. The charwoman stood grinning in the doorway as if she had good news to impart to the family but meant not to say a word unless properly questioned. The small ostrich feather standing upright on her hat, which had annoyed Mr. Samsa ever since she was engaged, was waving gaily in all directions. "Well, what is it then?" asked Mrs. Samsa, who obtained more respect from the charwoman than the others. "Oh," said the charwoman, giggling so amiably that she could not at once continue, "just this, you don't need to bother about how to get rid of the thing next door. It's been seen to already." Mrs. Samsa and Grete bent over their letters again, as if preoccupied; Mr. Samsa, who perceived that she was eager to begin describing it all in detail, stopped her with a decisive hand. But since she was not allowed to tell her story, she remembered the great hurry she was in, being obviously deeply huffed: "Bye, everybody," she said, whirling off violently, and departed with a frightful slamming of doors.

"She'll be given notice tonight," said Mr. Samsa, but neither from his wife nor his daughter did he get any answer, for the charwoman seemed to have shattered again the composure they had barely achieved. They rose, went to the window and stayed there, clasping each other tight. Mr. Samsa turned in his chair to look at them and quietly observed them for a little. Then he called out: "Come along, now, do. Let bygones be bygones. And you might have some consideration for me." The two of them complied at once, hastened to him, caressed him and quickly finished their letters.

Then they all left the apartment together, which was more than they had done for months, and went by tram into the open country outside the town. The tram, in which they were the only passengers, was filled with warm sunshine. Leaning comfortably back in their seats they canvassed their prospects for the future, and it appeared on closer inspection that these were not at all bad, for the jobs they had got, which so far they had never really dis-

cussed with each other, were all three admirable and likely to
lead to better things later on. The greatest immediate improvement in their condition would of course arise from moving to another house; they wanted to take a smaller and cheaper but also
better situated and more easily run apartment than the one they
had, which Gregor had selected. While they were thus conversing,
it struck both Mr. and Mrs. Samsa, almost at the same moment,
as they became aware of their daughter's increasing vivacity, that
in spite of all the sorrow of recent times, which had made her
cheeks pale, she had bloomed into a pretty girl with a good figure.
They grew quieter and half unconsciously exchanged glances of
complete agreement, having come to the conclusion that it would
soon be time to find a good husband for her. And it was like a
confirmation of their new dreams and excellent intentions that
at the end of their journey their daughter sprang to her feet first
and stretched her young body.

Ilse Aichinger

THE BOUND MAN

Sunlight on his face woke him, but made him shut his eyes again; it streamed unhindered down the slope, collected itself into rivulets, attracted swarms of flies, which flew low over his forehead, circled, sought to land, and were overtaken by fresh swarms. When he tried to whisk them away, he discovered that he was bound. A thick rope cut into his arms. He dropped them, opened his eyes again, and looked down at himself. His legs were tied all the way up to his thighs; a single length of rope was tied round his ankles, criss-crossed up his legs, and encircled his hips, his chest and his arms. He could not see where it was knotted. He showed no sign of fear or hurry, though he thought he was unable to move, until he discovered that the rope allowed his legs some free play and that round his body it was almost loose. His arms were tied to each other but not to his body, and had some free play too. This made him smile, and it occurred to him that perhaps children had been playing a practical joke on him.

He tried to feel for his knife, but again the rope cut softly into his flesh. He tried again, more cautiously this time, but his pocket was empty. Not only his knife, but the little money that he had on him, as well as his coat, were missing. His shoes had been pulled from his feet and taken too. When he moistened his lips he tasted blood, which had flowed from his temples down his cheeks, his chin, his neck, and under his shirt. His eyes were painful; if he kept them open for long he saw reddish stripes in the sky.

He decided to stand up. He drew his knees up as far as he

Translated by Eric Mosbacher. Reprinted with permission of Farrar, Straus & Giroux, Inc., from *The Bound Man and Other Stories* by Ilse Aichinger. Copyright 1956 by Ilse Aichinger. Published in England by Martin Secker & Warburg Limited.

could, rested his hands on the fresh grass and jerked himself to his feet. An elder branch stroked his cheek, the pain dazzled him, and the rope cut into his flesh. He collapsed to the ground again, half out of his mind with pain, and then tried again. He went on trying until the blood started flowing from his hidden weals. Then he lay still again for a long while and let the sun and the flies do what they liked.

When he awoke for the second time the elder bush had cast its shadow over him, and the coolness stored in it was pouring from between its branches. He must have been hit on the head. Then they must have laid him down carefully, just as a mother lays her baby behind a bush when she goes to work in the fields.

His chances all lay in the amount of free play allowed him by the rope. He dug his elbows into the ground and tested it. As soon as the rope tautened he stopped, and tried again more cautiously. If he had been able to reach the branch over his head he could have used it to drag himself to his feet, but he could not reach it. He laid his head back on the grass, rolled over, and struggled to his knees. He tested the ground with his toes, and then managed to stand up almost without effort.

A few paces away lay the path across the plateau, and in the grass were wild pinks and thistles in bloom. He tried to lift his foot to avoid trampling on them, but the rope round his ankles prevented him. He looked down at himself.

The rope was knotted at his ankles, and ran round his legs in a kind of playful pattern. He carefully bent and tried to loosen it, but, loose though it seemed to be, he could not make it any looser. To avoid treading on the thistles with his bare feet he hopped over them like a bird.

The cracking of a twig made him stop. People in this district were very prone to laughter. He was alarmed by the thought that he was in no position to defend himself. He hopped on until he reached the path. Bright fields stretched far below. He could see no sign of the nearest village, and if he could move no faster than this, night would fall before he reached it.

He tried walking and discovered that he could put one foot before another if he lifted each foot a definite distance from the ground and then put it down again before the rope tautened. In the same way he could actually swing his arms a little.

After the first step he fell. He fell right across the path, and made the dust fly. He expected this to be a sign for the long-suppressed laughter to break out, but all remained quiet. He was alone. As soon as the dust had settled he got up and went on. He looked down and watched the rope slacken, grow taut, and then slacken again.

When the first glow-worms appeared he managed to look up. He felt in control of himself again, and his impatience to reach the nearest village faded.

Hunger made him light-headed, and he seemed to be going so fast that not even a motorcycle could have overtaken him; alternatively he felt as if he were standing still and that the earth was rushing past him, like a river flowing past a man swimming against the stream. The stream carried branches which had been bent southward by the north wind, stunted young trees, and patches of grass with bright, long-stalked flowers. It ended by submerging the bushes and the young trees, leaving only the sky and the man above water level. The moon had risen, and illuminated the bare, curved summit of the plateau, the path, which was overgrown with young grass, the bound man making his way along it with quick, measured steps, and two hares, which ran across the hill just in front of him and vanished down the slope. Though the nights were still cool at this time of the year, before midnight the bound man lay down at the edge of the escarpment and went to sleep.

In the light of morning the animal-tamer who was camping with his circus in the field outside the village saw the bound man coming down the path, gazing thoughtfully at the ground. The bound man stopped and bent down. He held out one arm to help keep his balance and with the other picked up an empty wine-bottle. Then he straightened himself and stood erect again. He moved slowly, to avoid being cut by the rope, but to the circus proprietor what he did suggested the voluntary limitation of an enormous swiftness of movement. He was enchanted by its extraordinary gracefulness, and while the bound man looked about for a stone on which to break the bottle, so that he could use the splintered neck to cut the rope, the animal-tamer walked across the field and approached him. The first leaps of a young panther had never filled him with such delight.

"Ladies and gentlemen, the bound man!" His very first movements let loose a storm of applause, which out of sheer excitement caused the blood to rush to the cheeks of the animal-tamer standing at the edge of the arena. The bound man rose to his feet. His surprise whenever he did this was like that of a four-footed animal which has managed to stand on its hind legs. He knelt, stood up, jumped, and turned cartwheels. The spectators found it as astonishing as if they had seen a bird which voluntarily remained earthbound, and confined itself to hopping.

The bound man became an enormous draw. His absurd steps and little jumps, his elementary exercises in movement, made the rope dancer superfluous. His fame grew from village to village, but the motions he went through were few and always the same; they were really quite ordinary motions, which he had continually to practice in the daytime in the half-dark tent in order to retain his shackled freedom. In that he remained entirely within the limits set by his rope he was free of it, it did not confine him, but gave him wings and endowed his leaps and jumps with purpose; just as the flights of birds of passage have purpose when they take wing in the warmth of summer and hesitantly make small circles in the sky.

All the children of the neighborhood started playing the game of "bound man." They formed rival gangs, and one day the circus people found a little girl lying bound in a ditch, with a cord tied round her neck so that she could hardly breathe. They released her, and at the end of the performance that night the bound man made a speech. He announced briefly that there was no sense in being tied up in such a way that you could not jump. After that he was regarded as a comedian.

Grass and sunlight, tent pegs driven into the ground and then pulled up again, and on to the next village. "Ladies and gentlemen, the bound man!" The summer mounted toward its climax. It bent its face deeper over the fish ponds in the hollows, taking delight in its dark reflection, skimmed the surface of the rivers, and made the plain into what it was. Everyone who could walk went to see the bound man.

Many wanted a close-up view of how he was bound. So the circus proprietor announced after each performance that anyone who wanted to satisfy himself that the knots were real and the rope not made of rubber was at liberty to do so. The bound man generally waited for the crowd in the area outside the tent. He laughed or remained serious, and held out his arms for inspection. Many took the opportunity to look him in the face, others gravely tested the rope, tried the knots on his ankles, and wanted to know exactly how the lengths compared with the length of his limbs. They asked him how he had come to be tied up like that, and he answered patiently, always saying the same thing. Yes, he had been tied up, he said, and when he awoke he found that he had been robbed as well. Those who had done it must have been pressed for time, because they had tied him up somewhat too loosely for someone who was not supposed to be able to move and somewhat too tightly for someone who was expected to be able to move. But he did move, people pointed out. Yes, he replied, what else could he do?

Before he went to bed he always sat for a time in front of the fire. When the circus proprietor asked him why he didn't make up a better story he always answered that he hadn't made up that one, and blushed. He preferred staying in the shade.

The difference between him and the other performers was that when the show was over he did not take off his rope. The result was that every movement that he made was worth seeing, and the villagers used to hang about the camp for hours, just for the sake of seeing him get up from in front of the fire and roll himself in his blanket. Sometimes the sky was beginning to lighten when he saw their shadows disappear.

The circus proprietor often remarked that there was no reason why he should not be untied after the evening performance and tied up again next day. He pointed out that the rope dancers, for instance, did not stay on their rope overnight. But no one took the idea of untying him seriously.

For the bound man's fame rested on the fact that he was always bound, that whenever he washed himself he had to wash his clothes too and vice versa, and that his only way of doing so was to jump in the river just as he was every morning when the sun came out, and that he had to be careful not to go too far out for fear of being carried away by the stream.

The proprietor was well aware that what in the last resort protected the bound man from the jealousy of the other performers was his helplessness; he deliberately left them the pleasure of watching him groping painfully from stone to stone on the river bank every morning with his wet clothes clinging to him. When the proprietor's wife pointed out that even the best clothes would not stand up indefinitely to such treatment (and the bound man's clothes were by no means of the best), he replied curtly that it was not going to last forever. That was his answer to all objections—it was for the summer season only. But when he said this he was not being serious; he was talking like a gambler who has no intention of giving up his vice. In reality he would have been prepared cheerfully to sacrifice his lions and his rope dancers for the bound man.

He proved this on the night when the rope dancers jumped over the fire. Afterward he was convinced that they did it, not because it was midsummer's day, but because of the bound man, who as usual was lying and watching them with that peculiar smile that might have been real or might have been only the effect of the glow on his face. In any case no one knew anything about him because he never talked about anything that had happened to him before he emerged from the wood that day.

But that evening two of the performers suddenly picked him up by the arms and legs, carried him to the edge of the fire and started playfully swinging him to and fro, while two others held out their arms to catch him on the other side. In the end they threw him, but too short. The two men on the other side drew back—they explained afterward that they did so the better to take the shock. The result was that the bound man landed at the very edge of the flames and wound have been burned if the circus proprietor had not seized his arms and quickly dragged him away to save the rope which was starting to get singed. He was certain that the object had been to burn the rope. He sacked the four men on the spot.

A few nights later the proprietor's wife was awakened by the sound of footsteps on the grass, and went outside just in time to prevent the clown from playing his last practical joke. He was carrying a pair of scissors. When he was asked for an explanation he insisted that he had had no intention of taking the bound man's life, but only wanted to cut his rope because he felt sorry for him. He was sacked too.

These antics amused the bound man because he could have freed himself if he had wanted to whenever he liked, but perhaps he wanted to learn a few new jumps first. The children's rhyme: "We travel with the circus, we travel with the circus" sometimes occurred to him while he lay awake at night. He could hear the voices of spectators on the opposite bank who had been driven too far downstream on the way home. He could see the river gleaming in the moonlight, and the young shoots growing out of the thick tops of the willow trees, and did not think about autumn yet.

The circus proprietor dreaded the danger that sleep involved for the bound man. Attempts were continually made to release him while he slept. The chief culprits were sacked rope dancers, or children who were bribed for the purpose. But measures could be taken to safeguard against these. A much bigger danger was that which he represented to himself. In his dreams he forgot his rope, and was surprised by it when he woke in the darkness of morning. He would angrily try to get up, but lose his balance and fall back again. The previous evening's applause was forgotten, sleep was still too near, his head and neck too free. He was just the opposite of a hanged man—his neck was the only part of him that was free. You had to make sure that at such moments no knife was within his reach. In the early hours of the morning the circus proprietor sometimes sent his wife to see whether the bound man was all right. If he was asleep she would bend over him and feel the rope. It had grown hard from dirt and damp. She would test the amount of free play it allowed him, and touch his tender wrists and ankles.

The most varied rumors circulated about the bound man. Some said he had tied himself up and invented the story of having been robbed, and toward the end of the summer that was the general opinion. Others maintained that he had been tied up at his own request, perhaps in league with the circus proprietor. The hesitant way in which he told his story, his habit of breaking off when the talk got round to the attack on him, contributed greatly to these rumors. Those who still believed in the robbery-with-violence story were laughed at. Nobody knew what difficulties the circus proprietor had in keeping the bound man, and how often he said he had had enough and wanted to clear off, for too much of the summer had passed.

Later, however, he stopped talking about clearing off. When the proprietor's wife brought him his food by the river and asked him how long he proposed to remain with them, he did not answer. She thought he had got used, not to being tied up, but to remembering every moment that he was tied up—the only thing that anyone in his position could get used to. She asked him whether he did not think it ridiculous to be tied up all the time, but he answered that he did not. Such a variety of people—clowns, freaks, and comics, to say nothing of elephants and tigers—traveled with circuses that he did not see why a bound man should not travel with a circus too. He told her about the movements he was practicing, the new ones he had discovered, and about a new trick that had occurred to him while he was whisking flies from the animals' eyes. He described to her how he always anticipated the effect of the rope and always restrained his movements in such a way as to prevent it from ever tautening; and she knew that there were days when he was hardly aware of the rope, when he jumped down from the wagon and slapped the flanks of the horses in the morning as if he were moving in a dream. She watched him vault over the bars almost without touching them, and saw the sun on his face, and he told her that sometimes he felt as if he were not tied up at all. She answered that if he were prepared to be untied, there would never be any need for him to feel tied up. He agreed that he could be untied whenever he felt like it.

The woman ended by not knowing whether she was more concerned with the man or with the rope that tied him. She told him that he could go on traveling with the circus without his rope, but she did not believe it. For what would be the point of his antics without his rope, and what would he amount to without it? Without his rope he would leave them, and the happy days would be over. She would no longer be able to sit beside him on the stones by the river without arousing suspicion, and she knew that his continued presence, and her conversations with him, of which the rope was the only subject, depended on it. Whenever she agreed that the rope had its advantages, he would start talking about how troublesome it was, and whenever he started talking about its advantages, she would urge him to get rid of it. All this seemed as endless as the summer itself.

At other times she was worried at the thought that she was

herself hastening the end by her talk. Sometimes she would get up in the middle of the night and run across the grass to where he slept. She wanted to shake him, wake him up and ask him to keep the rope. But then she would see him lying there; he had thrown off his blanket, and there he lay like a corpse, with his legs outstretched and his arms close together, with the rope tied round them. His clothes had suffered from the heat and the water, but the rope had grown no thinner. She felt that he would go on traveling with the circus until the flesh fell from him and exposed the joints. Next morning she would plead with him more ardently than ever to get rid of his rope.

The increasing coolness of the weather gave her hope. Autumn was coming, and he would not be able to go on jumping into the river with his clothes on much longer. But the thought of losing his rope, about which he had felt indifferent earlier in the season, now depressed him.

The songs of the harvesters filled him with foreboding. "Summer has gone, summer has gone." But he realized that soon he would have to change his clothes, and he was certain that when he had been untied it would be impossible to tie him up again in exactly the same way. About this time the proprietor started talking about traveling south that year.

The heat changed without transition into quiet, dry cold, and the fire was kept going all day long. When the bound man jumped down from the wagon he felt the coldness of the grass under his feet. The stalks were bent with ripeness. The horses dreamed on their feet and the wild animals, crouching to leap even in their sleep, seemed to be collecting gloom under their skins which would break out later.

On one of these days a young wolf escaped. The circus proprietor kept quiet about it, to avoid spreading alarm, but the wolf soon started raiding cattle in the neighborhood. People at first believed that the wolf had been driven to these parts by the prospect of a severe winter, but the circus soon became suspect. The proprietor could not conceal the loss of the animal from his own employees, so the truth was bound to come out before long. The circus people offered the burgomasters of the neighboring villages their aid in tracking down the beast, but all their efforts were in vain. Eventually the circus was openly blamed for the damage and the danger, and spectators stayed away.

The bound man went on performing before half-empty seats without losing anything of his amazing freedom of movement. During the day he wandered among the surrounding hills under the thin-beaten silver of the autumn sky, and, whenever he could, lay down where the sun shone longest. Soon he found a place which the twilight reached last of all, and when at last it reached him he got up most unwillingly from the withered grass. In coming down the hill he had to pass through a little wood on its southern slope, and one evening he saw the gleam of two little green lights. He knew that they came from no church window, and was not for a moment under any illusion about what they were.

He stopped. The animal came toward him through the thinning foliage. He could make out its shape, the slant of its neck, its tail which swept the ground, and its receding head. If he had not been bound, perhaps he would have tried to run away, but as it was he did not even feel fear. He stood calmly with dangling arms and looked down at the wolf's bristling coat under which the muscles played like his own underneath the rope. He thought the evening wind was still between him and the wolf when the beast sprang. The man took care to obey his rope.

Moving with the deliberate care that he had so often put to the test, he seized the wolf by the throat. Tenderness for a fellow creature arose in him, tenderness for the upright being concealed in the four-footed. In a movement that resembled the drive of a great bird (he felt a sudden awareness that flying would be possible only if one were tied up in a special way) he flung himself at the animal and brought it to the ground. He felt a slight elation at having lost the fatal advantage of free limbs which causes men to be worsted.

The freedom he enjoyed in this struggle was having to adapt every movement of his limbs to the rope that tied him—the freedom of panthers, wolves, and the wild flowers that sway in the evening breeze. He ended up lying obliquely down the slope, clasping the animal's hind legs between his own bare feet and its head between his hands. He felt the gentleness of the faded foliage stroking the backs of his hands, and he felt his own grip almost effortlessly reaching its maximum, and he felt too how he was in no way hampered by the rope.

As he left the wood light rain began to fall and obscured the setting sun. He stopped for a while under the trees at the edge of the wood. Beyond the camp and the river he saw the fields where the cattle grazed, and the places where they crossed. Perhaps he would travel south with the circus after all. He laughed softly. It was against all reason. Even if he continued to put up with the sores that covered his joints and opened and bled when he made certain movements, his clothes would not stand up much longer to the friction of the rope.

The circus proprietor's wife tried to persuade her husband to announce the death of the wolf without mentioning that it had been killed by the bound man. She said that even at the time of his greatest popularity people would have refused to believe him capable of it, and in their present angry mood, with the nights getting cooler, they would be more incredulous than ever. The wolf had attacked a group of children at play that day, and nobody would believe that it had really been killed; for the circus proprietor had many wolves, and it was easy enough for him to hang a skin on the rail and allow free entry. But he was not to be dissuaded. He thought that the announcement of the bound man's act would revive the triumphs of the summer.

That evening the bound man's movements were uncertain. He stumbled in one of his jumps, and fell. Before he managed to get up he heard some low whistles and catcalls, rather like birds calling at dawn. He tried to get up too quickly, as he had done once or twice during the summer, with the result that he tautened the rope and fell back again. He lay still to regain his calm, and listened to the boos and catcalls growing into an uproar. "Well, bound man, and how did you kill the wolf?" they shouted, and: "Are you the man who killed the wolf?" If he had been one of them, he would not have believed it himself. He thought they had a perfect right to be angry: a circus at this time of year, a bound man, an escaped wolf, and all ending up with this. Some groups of spectators started arguing with others, but the greater part of the audience thought the whole thing a bad joke. By the time he had got to his feet there was such a hubbub that he was barely able to make out individual words.

He saw people surging up all round him, like faded leaves raised by a whirlwind in a circular valley at the center of which all was yet still. He thought of the golden sunsets of the last few days; and the sepulchral light which lay over the blight of all that he had built up during so many nights, the gold frame which the pious hang round dark, old pictures, this sudden collapse of everything, filled him with anger.

They wanted him to repeat his battle with the wolf. He said that such a thing had no place in a circus performance, and the proprietor declared that he did not keep animals to have them slaughtered in front of an audience. But the mob stormed the ring and forced them toward the cages. The proprietor's wife made her way between the seats to the exit and managed to get round to the cages from the other side. She pushed aside the attendant whom the crowd had forced to open a cage door, but the spectators dragged her back and prevented the door from being shut.

"Aren't you the woman who used to lie with him by the river in the summer?" they called out. "How does he hold you in his arms?" She shouted back at them that they needn't believe in the bound man if they didn't want to, they had never deserved him. Painted clowns were good enough for them.

The bound man felt as if the bursts of laughter were what he had been expecting ever since early May. What had smelt so sweet all through the summer now stank. But, if they insisted, he was ready to take on all the animals in the circus. He had never felt so much at one with his rope.

Gently he pushed the woman aside. Perhaps he would travel south with them after all. He stood in the open doorway of the cage, and he saw the wolf, a strong young animal, rise to its feet, and he heard the proprietor grumbling again about the loss of his exhibits. He clapped his hands to attract the animal's attention, and when it was near enough he turned to slam the cage door. He looked the woman in the face. Suddenly he remembered the proprietor's warning to suspect of murderous intentions anyone near him who had a sharp instrument in his hand. At the same moment he felt the blade on his wrists, as cool as the water of the river in autumn, which during the last few weeks he had been barely able to stand. The rope curled up in a tangle beside him while he struggled free. He pushed the woman back, but there was no point in anything he did now. Had he been insufficiently on his guard against those who wanted to release him, against the sympathy in which they wanted to lull him? Had he lain too long on the river bank? If she had cut the cord at any other moment it would have been better than this.

He stood in the middle of the cage, and rid himself of the rope like a snake discarding its skin. It amused him to see the spectators shrinking back. Did they realize that he had no choice now? Or that fighting the wolf now would prove nothing whatever? At the same time he felt all his blood rush to his feet. He felt suddenly weak.

The rope, which fell at its feet like a snare, angered the wolf more than the entry of a stranger into its cage. It crouched to spring. The man reeled, and grabbed the pistol that hung ready at the side of the cage. Then, before anyone could stop him, he shot the wolf between the eyes. The animal reared, and touched him in falling.

On the way to the river he heard the footsteps of his pursuers—spectators, the rope dancers, the circus proprietor, and the proprietor's wife, who persisted in the chase longer than anyone else. He hid in a clump of bushes and listened to them hurrying past, and later on streaming in the opposite direction back to the camp. The moon shone on the meadow; in that light its color was both of growth and of death.

When he came to the river his anger died away. At dawn it seemed to him as if lumps of ice were floating in the water, and as if snow had fallen, obliterating memory.

Cesare Pavese

SUICIDES

I

There are days when the city where I live wakes in the morning with a strange look. The people in the streets, the traffic, the trees—everything seems familiar but as if seen with new eyes, like those moments when one looks in the mirror and asks oneself: "Who is that man?" For me, those are the only days in the whole year that I really enjoy.

On such mornings I get away from the office a little early, if I can, and go down into the streets to mix with the crowd, staring unreservedly at everyone who goes by. One or two of them, I imagine, may stare at me in the same way, for in moments like this I really do feel a self-confidence that makes me quite a different man.

I am convinced that never in my whole life shall I have anything more precious than the revelation of how I can derive pleasure from these moments. One way of prolonging them that I have sometimes found successful is to sit in a modern-style café with wide, clear windows, and from that vantage point to savour the bustle on the pavements and in the streets, the whirl of colour, the babble of voices, and the inner calm that controls all this movement.

For some years, now, I have suffered from delusions and the bitterest remorse, yet I can affirm that my dearest wish is only for this peace, this serenity. I am not made for storms and struggles: and if, on certain mornings, I go down full of zest for a walk around the streets, and my past seems a perfidy, I repeat that I ask nothing more of life than being allowed to watch.

Translated by A. E. Murch. Reprinted from *Festival Night* by Cesare Pavese, by permission of Peter Owen Ltd.

Yet even this simple pleasure sometimes leaves me with the bitter after-taste one normally associates with a drug. Long ago I realised how essential astuteness is to living, and before being astute with others one must be astute with oneself. I envy those people who, before doing something wicked or grossly unfair, or even merely satisfying a selfish whim, manage to pre-arrange a chain of circumstances to make their action seem justifiable, even to their own consciences. Women are especially clever at this. I have no great vices (unless, indeed, my timorous shrinking from life's battle and my quest for serenity in solitude are the worst vices of all), but nevertheless I know how to be astute with myself and keep my self-control when I enjoy what little pleasure life allows me.

Sometimes I actually stop short in the street, look around me and wonder what right I have to enjoy such self-confidence. This frequently happens when I go out more often than usual. Not that I steal the time from my work; I maintain myself decently and support my niece at boarding school. (She is alone in the world and passes for my niece, but the old woman who calls herself my mother will not have her in the house). What I wonder is whether I am not being ridiculous when I stroll about so blissfully, staring at people; ridiculous and offensive. I sometimes think such pleasure is more than I deserve.

Or else, as happened the other morning, I may be sitting in a café and find myself watching some intriguing scene that first attracts my attention because the people taking part in it are so normal. Such an incident is quite enough to make me relapse into a guilt-stricken sense of loneliness, a prey to so many desolate memories. The more they recede into the past, the more does their unchanging life reveal their subtle, terrifying significance.

I watched five minutes of byplay between the young girl at the cash-desk and a customer in a light-coloured overcoat, who had a friend with him. The young man explained that the cashier owed him change from a hundred *lire* note. He banged on the desk, pretending to search his wallet and pockets. "That's not the way to treat clients, my girl," he said, winking at his embarrassed friend. The girl laughed, and the fellow invented a tale of the trips they would have taken taken together, with that hundred *lire*, up and down in the lift at the public convenience. With muffled bursts of laughter, they decided they would deposit those few *soldi* at the bank—when they got them.

"Goodbye, my girl," he called as he finally went out. "Think of me tonight." The cashier, laughing and excited, said to the waitress: "What a man!"

I had noticed that cashier on other mornings, and sometimes I smiled without looking at her, in a moment of forgetfulness. But my peace of mind is too fleeting; based on nothing. My customary remorse comes over me.

We are all dirty-minded in that way, but some of us can be genial about it, smiling and making others smile. Others keep it to themselves, letting it create a void inside them. After all, the first way is not so stupid as the second.

It is on mornings like this that I am surprised by the thought— and every time it strikes me afresh—that all I am really guilty of in life is stupidity. Others perhaps can do something wicked deliberately, with complete self-assurance, interesting themselves in their victim and in the game—and I suspect that a life spent in that way may give a great deal of satisfaction; as for me, all I have ever done is to suffer from a vast, inept lack of confidence, and to react against other people, when I come into contact with them, with stupid cruelty. That is why—and there's no remedy for it—it only needs a few moments of remorse and loneliness to overcome me, and my thoughts go back to Carlotta.

It's more than a year since she died, and by now I know all the ways in which the memory of her can take me by surprise. If I want to, I can even recognise the state of mind that initiates her reappearance and with a great effort distract myself. But I do not always want to. Even now, that remorse offers me dark angles to explore, new points that I scrutinize with the same anxiety and terror that I felt a year ago. I have been so true to her in my tortuous fashion that every one of those far-off days appears to my memory not as something fixed and unchangeable, but as an elusive impression that is to me as real as today.

Not that Carlotta had any mystery about her. She was, on the contrary, one of those women who are too simple, poor things, and grow worried if, for a moment, they stop being absolutely sincere and attempt a subterfuge or a touch of coquetry. But since they are simple, no one notices them. I have never understood how she could bear to earn her living working at a cash desk. She would have made an ideal sister.

What I still haven't fathomed, even today, is the way I felt about her, the restraint I had then. What, for instance, can I say about the evening when Carlotta had put on a velvet dress—an old one—to receive me in her little two-roomed apartment? I said I would have preferred her in a bathing costume. It was one of the first times I had called on her and I hadn't even kissed her yet.

However, Carlotta gave me a timid smile, went off into the other room and reappeared—incredibly—in a bathing costume. That was the evening when I kissed her for the first time and threw her down on the divan, but as soon as our lovemaking was finished I told her I always preferred to be alone afterwards and I went away. For three days I did not let her set eyes on me, and when I went back I addressed her formally in the third person.

So began a ridiculous love-affair, made up of timid confidences on her part and an occasional word or two on mine. Once, without thinking, I used the intimate "*tu*" as I spoke to her, but Carlotta did not respond. Then I asked if she had made it up with her husband. Carlotta answered tearfully, "He never treated me the way you do."

It was easy to make her lean her head on my breast while I caressed her and told her I loved her. Lonely as I was, why shouldn't I make love to that quasi-widow? And Carlotta gave in, softly confessing that she'd loved me from the first moment and thought I was an extraordinary man, but I had caused her a lot of unhappiness in the short time we had known each other; she didn't know why, but all the men treated her like that.

"When one is hot and one is cold," I smiled with my lips in her hair, "love will last."

Carlotta was pale; her enormous eyes often looked tired and strained. Her body was pale, too. That night, in the darkness of her room, she asked me if I had left her, that other time, because her body did not please me.

But I had no pity on her this time, either, and in the middle of the night I dressed myself and told her, without offering any excuses, that I had to get moving and go out. Carlotta wanted to go with me. "No," I said. "I like to be alone," and I left her with a kiss.

II

When I knew Carlotta, I was just recovering from a bitter blow that almost cost me my life; and I felt a grim amusement in going back through the deserted streets, fleeing from the one who loved me. It had so long been my lot to spend my nights and days humiliated and infuriated by a woman's caprice.

I am convinced, now, that no passion is powerful enough to change a man's true nature. Even the fear of death cannot alter his fundamental characteristics. Once the climax of passion is over one becomes again what one was before—honest man or rogue, father of a family or a mere boy—and lives one's own daily life. Or, rather, in the crisis one sees one's own true nature. It horrifies us, and normality disgusts us. The insult to us is so atrocious that we would rather be dead, but there is no-one to accuse us except ourselves. It is to that woman that I owe my present condition, reduced to a daily job with no scope and no hope of forging a closer link with the world at large, disliked by the next man, disliked by my mother whom I support, and by my "niece" whom I do not love. I owe it all to her. But would things have turned out differently with any other woman? Another, I mean, who would be capable of humiliating me as my nature demands?

Anyway, that was the thought that came to me whenever I had done something wrong, something that woman I loved could call faithless, and it gave me some comfort. At a certain stage of suffering we inevitably think we are suffering unjustly; it is a natural anaesthetic; it restores our energies, makes life as entertaining as we could possibly wish, fills us with a sense of our own importance in the face of things in general, flatters us. I have experienced it, and I could have wished that the injustice, the ingratitude, had been even more flagrant. In those long days and nights of anguish, I was conscious of a vague, secret awareness, like an atmosphere or a radiation. I remember my stunned amazement that it could have happened; that that woman was only a woman after all; that the delirium, the agony, the sighs, words, actions, even I myself, could all have turned out as they did.

So, having been treated unjustly, I revenged myself, not on the guilty one but on another woman, as happens in this world.

When I left Carlotta's apartment at night, after indulging my passion to the full, my mind was at ease. It pleased me to wander about by myself, feeling free to enjoy walking down that long avenue, vaguely recalling the sensations and the thoughts of my youth. I have always loved the simple pattern of the night. Street lamps alternating with zones of darkness evoke my most cherished flights of fancy, colouring and heightening them by the contrasts they present. Here I could give free play to the dull resentment I felt toward Carlotta because of her meekness and her lust, unhampered by the restraint I imposed on such thoughts, out of pity, while I was actually with her.

But I was no longer young. I tried to cut myself loose from Carlotta by reviewing in detail her body and her caresses, dispassionately. It seemed to me that, separated from her husband as she was, still young and childless, she might well fancy she had the right to turn to me as a refuge. But, poor girl, as a lover she was too naïve. Perhaps that was really why her husband was false to her.

I remember one evening when we were strolling arm in arm through the streets in the dusk on our way back from the cinema. Carlotta said: "I'm so happy. It's nice to go to the cinema with you."

"Did you ever go with your husband?"

Carlotta smiled: "Are you jealous?"

I shrugged. "What difference does it make?"

"I'm tired," she said, clinging to my arm. "This useless chain that binds us is ruining my life and his, too, and compels me to bear a name that has done me nothing but harm. It should be possible to get a divorce, at least when there are no children."

I felt affectionate that evening, from our long, warm contact and my rising desire. "Have you any scruples about it?" I asked.

"Oh, my dear," Carlotta sighed. "Why aren't you always as nice as you are tonight? Think . . . If I could get a divorce. . . ."

I said nothing. At one time, when she spoke to me of divorce I was shattered and exclaimed: "Please yourself. You're the best judge of that. Do what you like, and I'll bet you'll be awarded alimony, too, if it's true that he was unfaithful to you."

"I have never wanted anything," Carlotta replied. "Since that day I've been working," and she looked at me. "Now I've got you, I should think that I wasn't being fair to you if I took money from him."

That evening after the cinema, I closed her mouth with a kiss. Then I took her to the station café and gave her a couple of drinks. In the dim light from the windows we sat in a corner like a pair of lovers. I had several drinks myself and said to her, out loud, "Carlotta, let's get ourselves a child, tonight, shall we?"

People glanced at us as Carlotta, laughing and blushing, put her hand over my mouth.

I talked and talked. Carlotta spoke about the film, saying all sorts of silly things, passionately comparing us to the characters in the drama. I went on drinking, knowing that was the only way to make me feel loving towards Carlotta.

The cold air outside revived us and we ran to her home. I stayed with her all that night, and when I woke in the morning I felt her beside me, rumpled and drowsy. She stretched out her arms to embrace me and I did not repulse her. When I got up, though, my head was aching. I felt irritated by Carlotta's air of happiness as she prepared coffee for me, humming to herself. We both had to go out, but remembering the concierge she sent me on first, after kissing and hugging me behind the door.

My most vivid recollection of that awakening is of the trees in the street outside, their boughs stiff and dripping in the fog beyond the bedroom curtains. After all that warmth and affection inside, the keen air waiting for me out of doors stimulated my blood; only I would have rather stayed by myself, smoking and thinking, conjuring up a very different awakening and a different companion.

On these occasions Carlotta drew from me a tenderness that I reproached myself for, the moment I was alone again. I spent frenzied moments trying to purge my mind and free myself from even the faintest memory of her. Again I promised myself to be firmer, harsher, a promise I kept only too well. It must be clear that we made love out of boredom, lust, for any reason except the only one she tried to delude herself existed. It irritated me to recall her serene, blissful look after love-making. It made me furious to see it on her face, while the only woman from whom I wanted it had never given it to me.

"If you take me as I am, all right," I told her once, "but get it out of your head that you can be part of my life."

"Don't you love me?" Carlotta faltered.

"The little love I was capable of, I burned up when I was young."

But sometimes I grew angry at having admitted, out of shame or lust, that I loved her at all.

Carlotta tried to smile: "We are good friends, at least?"

"Listen," I told her seriously, "that sort of nonsense makes me sick: we are a man and a woman who bore each other, but we get on all right in bed. . . ."

"Oh, that, yes!" she cried, clutching my arm and hiding her face. "I like it, I like it!"

". . . and there's no more to it than that."

One such conversation, in which it seemed to me I had been weak, was enough to make me avoid her. If she telephoned me at the office from her café, I replied that I was busy. The first time this happened, Carlotta tried to take offence. Then I made her spend an evening of anguish by sitting coldly beside her on the divan. The shaded table lamp threw a white light over her knees, and from where I sat in the shadow I could feel the barely restrained passion of her glances. The tension was almost unbearable, and I myself broke it by remarking: "You should thank me, Signora: you will remember this session, perhaps more than many others."

Carlotta did not move, and I went on: "You'd like to murder me, Signora? Why not? But if you think you can act the lady with me, you're wasting your time. As for whims and fancies, I can produce those for myself." Carlotta was panting. "Not even a bathing costume," I told her, "will be any use to you tonight."

Carlotta leapt in front of me and I saw her dark head flash through the white light like a missile. I threw out my hands to ward her off, but she collapsed at my knees, weeping. I patted her on the head two or three times and rose to my feet. "I ought to cry, too, Carlotta, but I know it's no use. All you are feeling now, I've felt myself. I wanted to kill myself, but I lacked the courage. Here's the joke: one who is weak enough to think of suicide is too weak to do it . . . So get up, Carlotta, you'll be all right."

"Don't treat me like this," she sobbed.

"I'm not hurting you. And you know I like to be alone. If you let me go off by myself, I come back. Otherwise we shan't see each other again. Listen! Would you like me to love you?" She looked up, her face transfigured. "Then stop loving me. There's no other way. 'It's the hare that makes the hunter'."

Scenes like that shook Carlotta to her very roots, so much so that she thought of leaving me. (After all, didn't they show that our temperaments were basically similar?) Carlotta was fundamentally simple—too simple. She was incapable of realising this clearly, but certainly she felt it. She tried—poor, hapless creature—to mollify me by treating it lightly. "Such is life," she would say sometimes, and "Poor little me."

If she had thrown me over then, and stuck to it, I think I should have felt a little hurt. But Carlotta could not reject me. If I missed two evenings in a row, I found her with swollen eyes; and if sometimes, out of pity or tenderness, I stopped at the café and asked her to come out, she would jump up eagerly, confused and blushing, even pretty.

My bitterness did not trouble her; what did hurt her was any restraint, any resentment, that our intimacy tended to create in me. Since I did not love her, it seemed to me monstrous that she should have even the slightest claim on me. There were days when it made me shudder to address her as an intimate friend, an equal. I felt degraded. What was this woman to me, that she should take my arm?

To offset that mood, there were days when I felt reborn; times when I could leave work and walk in the fresh sunlight through the shining streets, free of her and of anything else, my body satisfied, my old griefs lulled to rest, eager to see, to savour, to feel as I did when I was young. The fact that Carlotta was suffering for love of me softened and alleviated my own by-gone sorrows, made me feel rather remote from them and from the mocking world. Away from her I found myself again, unharmed and more experienced. She was the sponge that had wiped me clean again. I often thought of her.

III

Some evenings when I talked and talked, absorbed in the game, I forgot my bitterness and became a boy again.

"Carlotta," I would say, "How are you off for lovers? It's a long time since I've been one of them, but, after all, that's the best way. If all goes well, one enjoys it; if badly, one hopes for better luck next time. They taught me to live a day at a time. How does that suit you, Carlotta?" She laughed and shook her head. "And then," I went on "they inspire such fine thoughts! The man we love—who couldn't care less—will never be as happy as we are. Unless . . . ," and I smiled, "he goes to bed with some other woman and gets his own back that way." Carlotta frowned. "Love's a fine thing," I concluded, "and nobody can escape it."

Carlotta served me as an audience. I talked on my own account, on those evenings, the best kind of talk. "There's love," I said, "and there's betrayal. To enjoy love to the full, it must also be a betrayal. That's a thing boys do not understand. You women learn it more quickly. Did you betray your husband?" Carlotta blushed and tried to smile.

"We boys were more stupid. We fell nobly in love with an actress or a girl-friend and devoted all our finest thoughts to her. Only we forgot to tell her about them. As far as I know, every girl of our age was already well aware that love is a problem of astuteness. It seems impossible, but boys go to the licensed brothels and conclude from that that the women outside are different. What did you do when you were sixteen, Carlotta?"

But Carlotta was thinking on different lines. Before she said a word, her eyes told me that I belonged to her. I hated the firm, possessive care for me that radiated from the look she gave me.

"What were you doing at sixteen?" I repeated, looking at the ground.

"Nothing," she replied gravely. I knew what she was thinking.

Then she asked my pardon, called herself a poor little thing, said she realised she had no right, but the gleam in her eyes was enough for me. "You're stupid, you know," I told her. "As far as I'm concerned, your husband could have you back," and I went away feeling relieved.

The next day but one, she phoned me timidly at the office and I replied curtly. In the evening we saw each other again.

Carlotta was amused when I told her about my school-girl niece, and shook her head incredulously when I said I would rather have sent my mother away to school and lived with the child. She imagined us as two beings living apart, pretending to be uncle and niece, but in reality sharing a whole world of absorbing secrets. She asked me scornfully if the girl wasn't really my daughter.

"Of course. She was born when I was sixteen. And she would be blonde, just to spite me. How can one manage to be born blonde? To me, fair-haired people are just animals, like monkeys or lions, as if they were always in the sun."

Carlotta remarked: "I was blonde, as a baby."

"I was bald," I replied.

In those last days I grew mildly curious about Carlotta's past, sometimes forgetting what she had already told me. I scanned her as one scans the gossip columns in the daily papers. I amused myself by puzzling her, asking her cruel questions and answering them myself. In reality, I was just listening to my own voice.

But Carlotta had understood me. "Tell me about yourself," she would say on some evenings, squeezing my arm. She knew that to make me talk about myself was the only way of keeping me as her friend.

"Have I ever told you, Carlotta," I said to her one night, "that a man killed himself because of me?" She looked at me, half smiling, half dismayed.

"It's nothing much to laugh at," I went on. "We died together, but he stayed that way. The dreams of youth . . ." (That's strange, I thought. I've never told anyone about it, and now I'm telling Carlotta.) "He was a friend of mine, a fine, fair-haired chap. He really did look like a lion. You girls never make friendships like that. You're already too jealous, even at that age. We went to school together, and always saw each other in the evenings. We talked filth, as boys do, but we were both in love with a lady. She must be living still. She was our first love, Carlotta. We spent our evening discussing love and death. No lover has ever been more certain of being understood by his friend than we were. Jean— that was his name—had a haughty sadness that put me to shame. All by himself he created the melancholy that pervaded those evenings we spent walking round in the fog. We had never believed one could suffer so much. . . ."

"Were you in love with her, too?"

"Jean was more unhappy than I was, and that troubled me. In the end I had the idea that we could kill ourselves and I told him about it. He thought it was a fine plan—he who was usually just a dreamer. We had only one revolver and we went into the hills to try it out in case it wouldn't work. Jean was the one who fired it. He had always been the leader in any adventure—indeed, I believe that if he hadn't fallen in love with that beautiful girl, I shouldn't have done so, either. We fired the gun—it was wintertime, and we were in a deserted lane half-way up the hillside—and I was still dazed by the violence of the explosion when Jean put the barrel into his mouth and said: 'This is how they do it!' The gun went off and killed him." Carlotta stared at me, shocked and terrified. "I did not know what to do," I said, "and I ran away."

That evening Carlotta asked me: "Did you really love that woman?"

"What woman? I loved Jean. I've already told you so."

"And did you feel like killing yourself, too?"

"Sure, I did. It would have been a silly thing to do, but it was terribly cowardly not to. I wish I had, sometimes."

Carlotta often recalled that story and talked to me about Jean as if she had known him. She made me describe him and asked me what I was like then. "Did you keep the revolver? Not to kill yourself, you know. Haven't you ever thought of killing yourself since?" She looked keenly at me as she spoke.

"Every time a man is in love he thinks of it."

Carlotta did not even smile. "D'you still think of it?"

"I think about Jean, sometimes."

IV

Carlotta put me to a lot of trouble at lunch-times. Going to and from my office I had to pass the windows of her café, and hide myself to avoid having to go in and cheer her up a bit. I did not go home at mid-day and I was only too glad to spend that little hour alone in some restaurant or other, smoking with my eyes half shut. Now and then I caught a glimpse of Carlotta perched on her stool, mechanically tearing off counterfoils, nodding, smiling or frowning, sometimes sharing a joke with a customer.

She was there from seven in the morning until four in the afternoon. She wore blue. They paid her four hundred and eighty *lire* a month, and Carlotta was quite happy to spend it all at once. For lunch she had a glass of milk, without leaving her desk. The job would have been easy enough, she used to tell me, if it hadn't been for the slamming of the door every time customers came in or went out. There were times when she felt it was battering on her brain.

After that, I shut the door carefully when I went into the café. When she was with me, Carlotta would try to describe to me those little scenes with the customers, but she couldn't manage to talk as I did, just as she failed to shock me with her suggestive hints about offers made to her by some lecherous old man or other.

"Get off with anybody you like," I told her, "only make sure I don't see him. Entertain him on the odd days. And watch out for V.D."

Carlotta gave a wry grimace. For some days she had had something on her mind. "In love again, Carlotta?" I asked her one evening, and she looked at me like a whipped dog. I began to lose patience with her, as I had before. The way her eyes shone in the darkness of her little room, the way she kept squeezing my hand, made me burn with anger. I was always afraid of getting too involved with her. I hated the very thought of it.

I grew sullen and boorish. But Carlotta no longer accepted my outbursts of bad temper with the submissive distress she used to show. She would stay quietly watching me, and sometimes she would gently withdraw from the caress I tried to give her to show I was sorry.

That pleased me even less. I found it repugnant to have to court her before I could possess her. The change did not come about suddenly, though. Carlotta would say: "I've got a headache . . . That door! Let's be good tonight. Talk to me."

When I realised that Carlotta was doing it intentionally, feeling humiliated and dredging up pangs of remorse, I stopped having those violent outbursts. I simply played her false. I started seeing again a woman I had known before, on those dreary evenings when, after visiting a brothel, I would sit and rest in some wretched café, feeling neither happy nor sad, just dazed. To me that seemed fair enough: either one accepts love with all its hazards or turns to the only other thing left—prostitution.

I thought Carlotta was pretending to be jealous and I laughed at her. She suffered, but she was too simple to turn her grief to good account. Instead, as happens to anyone who genuinely suffers, she lost her good looks. I was sorry about that, but I felt I should have to leave her.

Carlotta saw the blow coming. One night when we were in bed and I instinctively avoided any conversation, she suddenly pushed me away and curled herself up against the wall.

"What's the matter?" I asked crossly.

"If I were to disappear tomorrow," she said, suddenly turning round, "would it matter at all to you?"

"I don't know," I stammered.

"And if I betrayed you?"

"All life is a betrayal."

"And if I went back to my husband?" She meant what she said. I shrugged my shoulders. "I am a poor woman," she went on, "and I'm incapable of betraying you. I've seen my husband."

"How?"

"He came to the café."

"Didn't he skip off to Algeria, then?"

"I don't know," Carlotta replied. "I saw him at the café."

Perhaps she didn't mean to tell me, but it slipped out that her husband was with a woman in a fur coat. "Then you didn't get a chance to talk?" I asked.

Carlotta hesitated: "He came back the next day but one. He talked to me and brought me home."

I must admit I felt uneasy. "Here?" I asked softly.

Carlotta clung to me with her whole body. "But I love you," she murmured. "Don't imagine. . . ."

"Here?" I said again.

"It was nothing, dear. He talked to me about his business. Only, seeing him again, I realised how much I love you, and I wouldn't go back to him no matter how much he begged me."

"He did beg you, then?"

"No, but he told me that if he had to marry again, he'd marry me."

"Have you seen him since?"

"He came back to the café with that woman. . . ."

That was the last time I spent the night with Carlotta. Without saying goodbye to her, without regrets, I stopped running after

he had first seen the two men. They were no longer visible. Hence they must have tackled the rise. The sky was not so dark, for the snow had stopped falling during the night. The morning had opened with a dirty light which had scarcely become brighter as the ceiling of clouds lifted. At two in the afternoon it seemed as if the day were merely beginning. But still this was better than those three days when the thick snow was falling amidst unbroken darkness with little gusts of wind that rattled the double door of the classroom. Then Daru had spent long hours in his room, leaving it only to go to the shed and feed the chickens or get some coal. Fortunately the delivery truck from Tadjid, the nearest village to the north, had brought his supplies two days before the blizzard. It would return in forty-eight hours.

Besides, he had enough to resist a siege, for the little room was cluttered with bags of wheat that the administration left as a stock to distribute to those of his pupils whose families had suffered from the drought. Actually they had all been victims because they were all poor. Every day Daru would distribute a ration to the children. They had missed it, he knew, during these bad days. Possibly one of the fathers or big brothers would come this afternoon and he could supply them with grain. It was just a matter of carrying them over to the next harvest. Now shiploads of wheat were arriving from France and the worst was over. But it would be hard to forget that poverty, that army of ragged ghosts wandering in the sunlight, the plateaus burned to a cinder month after month, the earth shriveled up little by little, literally scorched, every stone bursting into dust under one's foot. The sheep had died then by thousands and even a few men, here and there, sometimes without anyone's knowing.

In contrast with such poverty, he who lived almost like a monk in his remote schoolhouse, nonetheless satisfied with the little he had and with the rough life, had felt like a lord with his white-washed walls, his narrow couch, his unpainted shelves, his well, and his weekly provision of water and food. And suddenly this snow, without warning, without the foretaste of rain. This is the way the region was, cruel to live in, even without men—who didn't help matters either. But Daru had been born here. Everywhere else, he felt exiled.

He stepped out onto the terrace in front of the schoolhouse. The two men were now halfway up the slope. He recognized the horseman as Balducci, the old gendarme he had known for a long time. Balducci was holding on the end of a rope an Arab who was walking behind him with hands bound and head lowered. The gendarme waved a greeting to which Daru did not reply, lost as he was in contemplation of the Arab dressed in a faded blue jellaba, his feet in sandals but covered with socks of heavy raw wool, his head surmounted by a narrow, short *chèche*. They were approaching. Balducci was holding back his horse in order not to hurt the Arab, and the group was advancing slowly.

Within earshot, Balducci shouted: "One hour to do the three kilometers from El Ameur!" Daru did not answer. Short and square in his thick sweater, he watched them climb. Not once had the Arab raised his head. "Hello," said Daru when they got up onto the terrace. "Come in and warm up." Balducci painfully got down from his horse without letting go of the rope. From under his bristling mustache he smiled at the schoolmaster. His little dark eyes, deep-set under a tanned forehead, and his mouth surrounded with wrinkles made him look attentive and studious. Daru took the bridle, led the horse to the shed, and came back to the two men, who were now waiting for him in the school. He led them into his room. "I am going to heat up the classroom," he said. "We'll be more comfortable there." When he entered the room again, Balducci was on the couch. He had undone the rope tying him to the Arab, who had squatted near the stove. His hands still bound, the *chèche* pushed back on his head, he was looking toward the window. At first Daru noticed only his huge lips, fat, smooth, almost Negroid; yet his nose was straight, his eyes were dark and full of fever. The *chèche* revealed an obstinate forehead and, under the weathered skin now rather discolored by the cold, the whole face had a restless and rebellious look that struck Daru when the Arab, turning his face toward him, looked him straight in the eyes. "Go into the other room," said the schoolmaster, "and I'll make you some mint tea." "Thanks," Balducci said. "What a chore! How I long for retirement." And addressing his prisoner in Arabic: "Come on, you." The Arab got up and, slowly, holding his bound wrists in front of him, went into the classroom.

With the tea, Daru brought a chair. But Balducci was already enthroned on the nearest pupil's desk and the Arab had squatted against the teacher's platform facing the stove, which stood between the desk and the window. When he held out the glass of tea to the prisoner, Daru hesitated at the sight of his bound hands. "He might perhaps be untied." "Sure," said Balducci. "That was for the trip." He started to get to his feet. But Daru, setting the glass on the floor, had knelt beside the Arab. Without saying anything, the Arab watched him with his feverish eyes. Once his hands were free, he rubbed his swollen wrists against each other, took the glass of tea, and sucked up the burning liquid in swift little sips.

"Good," said Daru. "And where are you headed?"

Balducci withdrew his mustache from the tea. "Here, son."

"Odd pupils! And you're spending the night?"

"No. I'm going back to El Ameur. And you will deliver this

fellow to Tinguit. He is expected at police headquarters."

Balducci was looking at Daru with a friendly little smile.

"What's this story?" asked the schoolmaster. "Are you pulling my leg?"

"No, son. Those are the orders."

"The orders? I'm not . . ." Daru hesitated, not wanting to hurt the old Corsican. "I mean, that's not my job."

"What! What's the meaning of that? In wartime people do all kinds of jobs."

"Then I'll wait for the declaration of war!"

Balducci nodded.

"O.K. But the orders exist and they concern you too. Things are brewing, it appears. There is talk of a forthcoming revolt. We are mobilized, in a way."

Daru still had his obstinate look.

"Listen, son," Balducci said. "I like you and you must understand. There's only a dozen of us at El Ameur to patrol throughout the whole territory of a small department and I must get back in a hurry. I was told to hand this guy over to you and return without delay. He couldn't be kept there. His village was beginning to stir; they wanted to take him back. You must take him to Tinguit tomorrow before the day is over. Twenty kilometers shouldn't faze a husky fellow like you. After that, all will be over. You'll come back to your pupils and your comfortable life."

Behind the wall the horse could be heard snorting and pawing the earth. Daru was looking out the window. Decidedly, the weather was clearing and the light was increasing over the snowy plateau. When all the snow was melted, the sun would take over again and once more would burn the fields of stone. For days, still, the unchanging sky would shed its dry light on the solitary expanse where nothing had any connection with man.

"After all," he said, turning around toward Balducci, "what did he do?" And, before the gendarme had opened his mouth, he asked: "Does he speak French?"

"No, not a word. We had been looking for him for a month, but they were hiding him. He killed his cousin."

"Is he against us?"

"I don't think so. But you can never be sure."

"Why did he kill?"

"A family squabble, I think. One owed the other grain, it seems. It's not at all clear. In short, he killed his cousin with a billhook. You know, like a sheep, *kreezk!*"

Balducci made the gesture of drawing a blade across his throat and the Arab, his attention attracted, watched him with a sort of anxiety. Daru felt a sudden wrath against the man, against all men with their rotten spite, their tireless hates, their blood lust.

But the kettle was singing on the stove. He served Balducci more tea, hesitated, then served the Arab again, who, a second time, drank avidly. His raised arms made the jellaba fall open and the schoolmaster saw his thin, muscular chest.

"Thanks, kid," Balducci said. "And now, I'm off."

He got up and went toward the Arab, taking a small rope from his pocket.

"What are you doing?" Daru asked dryly.

Balducci, disconcerted, showed him the rope.

"Don't bother."

The old gendarme hesitated. "It's up to you. Of course, you are armed?"

"I have my shotgun."

"Where?"

"In the trunk."

"You ought to have it near your bed."

"Why? I have nothing to fear."

"You're crazy, son. If there's an uprising, no one is safe, we're all in the same boat."

"I'll defend myself. I'll have time to see them coming."

Balducci began to laugh, then suddenly the mustache covered the white teeth. "You'll have time? O.K. That's just what I was saying. You have always been a little cracked. That's why I like you, my son was like that."

At the same time he took out his revolver and put in on the desk.

"Keep it; I don't need two weapons from here to El Ameur."

The revolver shone against the black paint of the table. When the gendarme turned toward him, the schoolmaster caught the smell of leather and horseflesh.

"Listen, Balducci," Daru said suddenly, "every bit of this disgusts me, and first of all your fellow here. But I won't hand him over. Fight, yes, if I have to. But not that."

The old gendarme stood in front of him and looked at him severely.

"You're being a fool," he said slowly. "I don't like it either. You don't get used to putting a rope on a man even after years of it, and you're even ashamed—yes, ashamed. But you can't let them have their way."

"I won't hand him over," Daru said again.

"It's an order, son, and I repeat it."

"That's right. Repeat to them what I've said to you: I won't hand him over."

Balducci made a visible effort to reflect. He looked at the Arab and at Daru. At last he decided.

"No, I won't tell them anything. If you want to drop us, go

ahead; I'll not denounce you. I have an order to deliver the prisoner and I'm doing so. And now you'll just sign this paper for me."

"There's no need. I'll not deny that you left him with me."

"Don't be mean with me. I know you'll tell the truth. You're from hereabouts and you are a man. But you must sign, that's the rule."

Daru opened his drawer, took out a little square bottle of purple ink, the red wooden penholder with the "sergeant-major" pen he used for making models of penmanship, and signed. The gendarme carefully folded the paper and put it into his wallet. Then he moved toward the door.

"I'll see you off," Daru said.

"No," said Balducci. "There's no use being polite. You insulted me."

He looked at the Arab, motionless in the same spot, sniffed peevishly, and turned away toward the door. "Good-by, son," he said. The door shut behind him. Balducci appeared outside the window and then disappeared. His footsteps were muffled by the snow. The horse stirred on the other side of the wall and several chickens fluttered in fright. A moment later Balducci reappeared outside the window leading the horse by the bridle. He walked toward the little rise without turning around and disappeared from sight with the horse following him. A big stone could be heard bouncing down. Daru walked back toward the prisoner, who, without stirring, never took his eyes off him. "Wait," the schoolmaster said in Arabic and went toward the bedroom. As he was going through the door, he had a second thought, went to the desk, took the revolver, and stuck it in his pocket. Then, without looking back, he went into his room.

For some time he lay on his couch watching the sky gradually close over, listening to the silence. It was this silence that had seemed painful to him during the first days here, after the war. He had requested a post in the little town at the base of the foothills separating the upper plateaus from the desert. There, rocky walls, green and black to the north, pink and lavender to the south, marked the frontier of eternal summer. He had been named to a post farther north, on the plateau itself. In the beginning, the solitude and the silence had been hard for him on these wastelands peopled only by stones. Occasionally, furrows suggested cultivation, but they had been dug to uncover a certain kind of stone good for building. The only plowing here was to harvest rocks. Elsewhere a thin layer of soil accumulated in the hollows would be scraped out to enrich paltry village gardens. This is the way it was: bare rock covered three quarters of the region. Towns sprang up, flourished, then disappeared; men came by, loved one another or fought bitterly, then died. No one in this desert, neither he nor his guest, mattered. And yet, outside this desert neither of them, Daru knew, could have really lived.

When he got up, no noise came from the classroom. He was amazed at the unmixed joy he derived from the mere thought that the Arab might have fled and that he would be alone with no decision to make. But the prisoner was there. He had merely stretched out between the stove and the desk. With eyes open, he was staring at the ceiling. In that position, his thick lips were particularly noticeable, giving him a pouting look. "Come," said Daru. The Arab got up and followed him. In the bedroom, the schoolmaster pointed to a chair near the table under the window. The Arab sat down without taking his eyes off Daru.

"Are you hungry?"

"Yes," the prisoner said.

Daru set the table for two. He took flour and oil, shaped a cake in a frying-pan, and lighted the little stove that functioned on bottled gas. While the cake was cooking, he went out to the shed to get cheese, eggs, dates, and condensed milk. When the cake was done he set it on the window sill to cool, heated some condensed milk diluted with water, and beat up the eggs into an omelette. In one of his motions he knocked against the revolver stuck in his right pocket. He set the bowl down, went into the classroom, and put the revolver in his desk drawer. When he came back to the room, night was falling. He put on the light and served the Arab. "Eat," he said. The Arab took a piece of the cake, lifted it eagerly to his mouth, and stopped short.

"And you?" he asked.

"After you. I'll eat too."

The thick lips opened slightly. The Arab hesitated, then bit into the cake determinedly.

The meal over, the Arab looked at the schoolmaster. "Are you the judge?"

"No, I'm simply keeping you until tomorrow."

"Why do you eat with me?"

"I'm hungry."

The Arab fell silent. Daru got up and went out. He brought back a folding bed from the shed, set it up between the table and the stove, perpendicular to his own bed. From a large suitcase which, upright in a corner, served as a shelf for papers, he took two blankets and arranged them on the camp bed. Then he stopped, felt useless, and sat down on his bed. There was nothing more to do or to get ready. He had to look at this man. He looked at him, therefore, trying to imagine his face bursting with rage. He couldn't do so. He could see nothing but the dark yet shining eyes and the animal mouth.

"Why did you kill him?" he asked in a voice whose hostile tone surprised him.

The Arab looked away. "He ran away. I ran after him."

He raised his eyes to Daru again and they were full of a sort of woeful interrogation. "Now what will they do to me?"

"Are you afraid?"

He stiffened, turning his eyes away.

"Are you sorry?"

The Arab stared at him openmouthed. Obviously he did not understand. Daru's annoyance was growing. At the same time he felt awkward and self-conscious with his big body wedged between the two beds.

"Lie down there," he said impatiently. "That's your bed."

The Arab didn't move. He called to Daru:

"Tell me!"

The schoolmaster looked at him.

"Is the gendarme coming back tomorrow?"

"I don't know."

"Are you coming with us?"

"I don't know. Why?"

The prisoner got up and stretched out on top of the blankets, his feet toward the window. The light from the electric bulb shone straight into his eyes and he closed them at once.

"Why?" Daru repeated, standing beside the bed.

The Arab opened his eyes under the blinding light and looked at him, trying not to blink.

"Come with us," he said.

In the middle of the night, Daru was still not asleep. He had gone to bed after undressing completely; he generally slept naked. But when he suddenly realized that he had nothing on, he hesitated. He felt vulnerable and the temptation came to him to put his clothes back on. Then he shrugged his shoulders; after all, he wasn't a child and, if need be, he could break his adversary in two. From his bed he could observe him, lying on his back, still motionless with his eyes closed under the harsh light. When Daru turned out the light, the darkness seemed to coagulate all of a sudden. Little by little, the night came back to life in the window where the starless sky was stirring gently. The schoolmaster soon made out the body lying at his feet. The Arab still did not move, but his eyes seemed open. A faint wind was prowling around the schoolhouse. Perhaps it would drive away the clouds and the sun would reappear.

During the night the wind increased. The hens fluttered a little and then were silent. The Arab turned over on his side with his back to Daru, who thought he heard him moan. Then he listened for his guest's breathing, become heavier and more regular. He listened to that breath so close to him and mused without being able to go to sleep. In this room where he had been sleeping alone for a year, this presence bothered him. But it bothered him also by imposing on him a sort of brotherhood he knew well but refused to accept in the present circumstances. Men who share the same rooms, soldiers or prisoners, develop a strange alliance as if, having cast off their armor with their clothing, they fraternized every evening, over and above their differences, in the ancient community of dream and fatigue. But Daru shook himself; he didn't like such musings, and it was essential to sleep.

A little later, however, when the Arab stirred slightly, the schoolmaster was still not asleep. When the prisoner made a second move, he stiffened, on the alert. The Arab was lifting himself slowly on his arms with almost the motion of a sleepwalker. Seated upright in bed, he waited motionless without turning his head toward Daru, as if he were listening attentively. Daru did not stir; it had just occurred to him that the revolver was still in the drawer of his desk. It was better to act at once. Yet he continued to observe the prisoner, who, with the same slithery motion, put his feet on the ground, waited again, then began to stand up slowly. Daru was about to call out to him when the Arab began to walk, in a quite natural but extraordinary silent way. He was heading toward the door at the end of the room that opened into the shed. He lifted the latch with precaution and went out, pushing the door behind him but without shutting it. Daru had not stirred. "He is running away," he merely thought. "Good riddance!" Yet he listened attentively. The hens were not fluttering; the guest must be on the plateau. A faint sound of water reached him, and he didn't know what it was until the Arab again stood framed in the doorway, closed the door carefully, and came back to bed without a sound. Then Daru turned his back on him and fell asleep. Still later he seemed, from the depths of his sleep, to hear furtive steps around the schoolhouse. "I'm dreaming! I'm dreaming!" he repeated to himself. And he went on sleeping.

When he awoke, the sky was clear; the loose window let in a cold, pure air. The Arab was asleep, hunched up under the blankets now, his mouth open, utterly relaxed. But when Daru shook him, he started dreadfully, staring at Daru with wild eyes as if he had never seen him and such a frightened expression that the schoolmaster stepped back. "Don't be afraid. It's me. You must eat." The Arab nodded his head and said yes. Calm had returned to his face, but his expression was vacant and listless.

The coffee was ready. They drank it seated together on the folding bed as they munched their pieces of the cake. Then Daru led the Arab under the shed and showed him the faucet where he washed. He went back into the room, folded the blankets and the bed, made his own bed and put the room in order. Then he went through the classroom and out onto the terrace. The sun was already rising in the blue sky; a soft, bright light was bathing the deserted plateau. On the ridge the snow was melting in spots. The stones were about to reappear. Crouched on the edge of the plateau, the schoolmaster looked at the deserted expanse. He thought of Balducci. He had hurt him, for he had sent him off in a way as if he didn't want to be associated with him. He could still hear the gendarme's farewell and, without knowing why, he felt strangely empty and vulnerable. At that moment, from the other side of the schoolhouse, the prisoner coughed. Daru listened to him almost despite himself and then, furious, threw a pebble that whistled through the air before sinking into the snow. That man's stupid crime revolted him, but to hand him over was contrary to honor. Merely thinking of it made him smart with humiliation. And he cursed at one and the same time his own people who had sent him this Arab and the Arab too who had dared to kill and not managed to get away. Daru got up, walked in a circle on the terrace, waited motionless, and then went back into the schoolhouse.

The Arab, leaning over the cement floor of the shed, was washing his teeth with two fingers. Daru looked at him and said: "Come." He went back into the room ahead of the prisoner. He slipped a hunting-jacket on over his sweater and put on walking-shoes. Standing, he waited until the Arab had put on his *chèche* and sandals. They went into the classroom and the schoolmaster pointed to the exit, saying: "Go ahead." The fellow didn't budge. "I'm coming," said Daru. The Arab went out. Daru went back into the room and made a package of pieces of rusk, dates, and sugar. In the classroom, before going out, he hesitated a second in front of his desk, then crossed the threshold and locked the door. "That's the way," he said. He started toward the east, followed by the prisoner. But, a short distance from the schoolhouse, he thought he heard a slight sound behind them. He retraced his steps and examined the surroundings of the house; there was no one there. The Arab watched him without seeming to understand. "Come on," said Daru.

They walked for an hour and rested beside a sharp peak of limestone. The snow was melting faster and faster and the sun was drinking up the puddles at once, rapidly cleaning the plateau, which gradually dried and vibrated like the air itself. When they resumed walking, the ground rang under their feet. From time to time a bird rent the space in front of them with a joyful cry. Daru breathed in deeply the fresh morning light. He felt a sort of rapture before the vast familiar expanse, now almost entirely yellow under its dome of blue sky. They walked an hour more, descending toward the south. They reached a level height made up of crumbly rocks. From there on, the plateau sloped down, eastward toward a low plain where there were a few spindly trees and, to the south, toward outcroppings of rock that gave the landscape a chaotic look.

Daru surveyed the two directions. There was nothing but the sky on the horizon. Not a man could be seen. He turned toward the Arab, who was looking at him blankly. Daru held out the package to him. "Take it," he said. "There are dates, bread, and sugar. You can hold out for two days. Here are a thousand francs too." The Arab took the package and the money but kept his full hands at chest level as if he didn't know what to do with what was being given him. "Now look," the schoolmaster said as he pointed in the direction of the east, "there's the way to Tinguit. You have a two-hour walk. At Tinguit you'll find the administration and the police. They are expecting you." The Arab looked toward the east, still holding the package and the money against his chest. Daru took his elbow and turned him rather roughly toward the south. At the foot of the height on which they stood could be seen a faint path. "That's the trail across the plateau. In a day's walk from here you'll find pasturelands and the first nomads. They'll take you in and shelter you according to their law." The Arab had now turned toward Daru and a sort of panic was visible in his expression. "Listen," he said. Daru shook his head: "No, be quiet. Now I'm leaving you." He turned his back on him, took two long steps in the direction of the school, looked hesitantly at the motionless Arab, and started off again. For a few minutes he heard nothing but his own step resounding on the cold ground and did not turn his head. A moment later, however, he turned around. The Arab was still there on the edge of the hill, his arms hanging now, and he was looking at the schoolmaster. Daru felt something rise in his throat. But he swore with impatience, waved vaguely, and started off again. He had already gone some distance when he again stopped and looked. There was no longer anyone on the hill.

Daru hesitated. The sun was now rather high in the sky and was beginning to beat down on his head. The schoolmaster retraced his steps, at first somewhat uncertainly, then with decision. When he reached the little hill, he was bathed in sweat. He climbed it as fast as he could and stopped, out of breath, at the top. The rock-fields to the south stood out sharply against the blue sky, but on the plain to the east a steamy heat was already rising. And in that slight haze, Daru, with heavy heart, made out the Arab walking slowly on the road to prison.

A little later, standing before the window of the classroom, the schoolmaster was watching the clear light bathing the whole surface of the plateau, but he hardly saw it. Behind him on the blackboard, among the winding French rivers, sprawled the clumsily chalked-up words he had just read: "You handed over our brother. You will pay for this." Daru looked at the sky, the plateau, and, beyond, the invisible lands stretching all the way to the sea. In this vast landscape he had loved so much, he was alone.

Luigi Pirandello

A DAY GOES BY

Rudely awakened from sleep—perhaps by mistake—I find myself thrown out of the train at a station along the line. It's night time. I've got nothing with me.

I can't get over my bewilderment. But what strikes me most forcibly is that nowhere on myself can I find any sign of the violence I've suffered. Not only this. I have no picture in my mind of its happening, not even the shadow of a memory.

I find myself on the ground, alone, in the shadowy darkness of a deserted station, and I don't know who it is I ought to ask, if I'm to find out where I am and what's happened to me.

I only got a quick glimpse of a small bull's-eye lantern which rushed forward to close the carriage-door through which I'd been ejected. The train had left immediately. And that lamp had immediately disappeared again into the inside of the station, its wobbling, flickering light struggling fruitlessly with the blackness. I was so utterly astounded by everything that it hadn't so much as passed through my mind that I might rush after it to demand an explanation and lodge my formal complaint.

But, formal complaint about *what*?

With boundless dismay I perceive that I no longer have the faintest memory of having started off on a journey by train. I haven't the slightest memory of where I started from, or where I was going to. Or if, on leaving, I really had anything with me. I had nothing, I think.

In the emptiness of this horrible uncertainty, I'm suddenly seized with terror at that spectral lantern which had immediately retreated from the scene, without paying the slightest attention to my being ejected from the train. Am I to deduce that it's the most

Translated by Frederick May. From *Luigi Pirandello: Short Stories*, translated and edited by Frederick May, © 1965, by permission of The Pirandello Estate.

natural thing in the world for people to get out at this station in that particular way?

In the darkness I have no luck with my attempts to decipher the name of the station. The town, however, is quite definitely one I don't know. In the first grey, feeble rays of the rising sun it looks deserted. In the vast pale square in front of the station there's a street lamp still alight. I move over to it. I stop and, not daring to raise my eyes—so terrified am I by the echo roused by my footsteps in the silence—I look at my hands, I look at the fronts, I look at the backs. I clench them, I open them again. I tap and prod myself with them, I feel myself all over. I even work out how I'm made, because I can't even be certain of this any longer—that I really exist and that all this is true.

Shortly afterwards, as I penetrate farther and farther into the city centre, at every step I see things that would bring me to a standstill with utter amazement, if an even greater amazement didn't overcome me. I observe that all the other people—they all look like me, too—are moving along, weaving in and out past one another, without paying one another the slightest attention; as if, so far as they're concerned, this is the most natural and usual thing in the world for them to do. I feel as if I were being drawn along—but, here again, without getting the sensation that anyone's using violence on me. It's just that I, within myself, ignorant of everything as I am—well, it's as if I were being held somehow on every side. But I consider that, even if I don't even know how, or whence, or why I've come there, *I* must be in the wrong, and the others must quite assuredly be in the right. Not only do they seem to know this, but they also know everything that makes them sure that they never make a mistake. They're without the slightest hesitancy, so naturally convinced are they that they must do what they're doing. So I'd certainly attract their wonder, their apprehension, perhaps even their indignation if, either because of the way they look or because of some action or expression of theirs, I started laughing or showed how utterly astounded I was. In my acute desire to find out something, without making myself look conspicuous, I have continually to obliterate from my eyes that something akin to irritability which you quite often see fleetingly in dogs' eyes. I'm in the wrong—I'm the one who's in the wrong, if I don't understand a thing, if I still can't succeed in pulling myself together again. I must make an effort and pretend that I too am quite convinced. I must contrive to act like the others, however much I'm lacking in all criteria by which to appraise, and any practical notion even of those things which seem most commonplace and easy.

I don't know in which role to re-establish myself, which path to take, or what to start doing.

Is it possible, however, that I've grown as big as I have, yet remained all the time like a child, without ever having done anything? Perhaps it's only been in a dream that I've worked. I don't know how. But I certainly *have* worked. I've always worked, worked very hard, very hard indeed. It looks as if everyone knows it, moreover, because lots and lots of people turn round and look at me, and more than one of them even goes so far as to wave to me. I don't know them, though. At first I just stand there, looking perplexed, wondering if that wave was really meant for me. I look to either side of me. I look behind me. Were they, possibly, waving to me by mistake? No, no, they really were waving to me. I struggle (in some embarrassment) with a certain vanity, which would dearly like me to deceive myself. It doesn't succeed, though. I move on as if I were suspended in mid-air, without being able to free myself from a strange sense of oppression which derives from something that is—and I recognize it as such—really quite wretched. I'm not at all sure about the suit I've got on. It seems odd that it should be mine. And now I've got a suspicion that it's this suit they're waving at and not me. And, just to make things really troublesome, I haven't got anything else with me except this suit!

I start feeling about myself again. I get a surprise. I can feel something like a small leather wallet tucked away in the breast pocket of the jacket. I fish it out, practically certain in my own mind that it doesn't belong to me but to this suit that isn't mine. It really is a small leather wallet, a faded yellow in colour—with a washed-out look about it, as if it had fallen into a stream or down a well and then been fished out of the water again. I open it—or rather, I unstick two bits of it that have got stuck together—and look inside. Buried among few folded sheets of paper, which the water has rendered illegible by staining them and making the ink run, I find a small holy picture—the sort they give children in church. It's all yellowed with age, and attached to it there's a photograph, almost of the same format and just as faded as it is. I detach it and study it. Oh! It's the photograph of a beautiful young woman in a bathing costume. She's almost naked. The wind is blowing strongly through her hair, and her arms are raised in a vivacious gesture of greeting. As I gaze at her—admiringly, yet with a certain feeling of pain (I don't know quite how to describe it, it's as if it came from far, far away)—I sense, coming from her, the impression, if not exactly the certainty, that the greeting waved by those arms is directed at me. But, no matter how hard I try, I can't recognize her. Is it even remotely possible that so lovely a woman as she can have slipped my memory? Perhaps she's been carried away by all that wind which is ruffling her hair. One thing's quite definite: in that leather wallet, which at some time in the past fell into the water, this picture, side by side with the holy picture, is in the place where you put your fiancée's photograph.

I resume my rummaging through the envelope and, more disconcerted than pleased—because I'm very doubtful about whether it belongs to me—I find a huge banknote tucked away in a secret hiding-place. Heaven only knows how long ago it was put there and forgotten. It's folded in four, all worn with use and here and there on the back it's so cracked by folds that it's positively threadbare.

Unprovided as I am with anything, can I provide myself with a little help by using it? I don't know with quite what strength of conviction, but the woman portrayed in that little photograph assures me that the banknote's mine. But can you really trust a charming little head like that, so ruffled by the wind? It's already past midday. I'm dropping with weariness. I must have something to eat. I go into a restaurant.

To my amazement I find myself greeted like an honoured guest. I'm obviously most welcome. I'm shown to a table that's already laid, a chair is drawn aside and I'm invited to take a seat. A scruple holds me back, however. I signal to the proprietor and, drawing him to one side, I show him the huge threadbare banknote. He gazes at it in utter astonishment. He examines it, filled with compassion for the condition to which it's been reduced. Then he tells me that it's undoubtedly of great value, but that it's one of a series which was withdrawn from circulation some time ago. I'm not to worry, however. If it's presented at the bank by someone as important and respectable as myself, it will certainly be accepted and changed into notes of smaller denomination which are currently legal tender.

Saying this, the proprietor of the restaurant accompanies me to the door and out on to the pavement, where he points out the nearby building that houses the bank.

I go in, and everyone in the bank is just as happy to do me this favour. That banknote of mine, they tell me, is one of the very few of that series not yet returned to the bank. For some time now, in this part of the country, they've no longer been putting into circulation notes other than those of minute size. They give me masses and masses of them, so that I feel embarrassed, even oppressed by them. I've only got that shipwrecked leather wallet with me. But they urge me not to let myself get worried. There's a remedy for everything. I can leave that money of mine in the bank, in a current account. I pretend I've understood. I put some of the notes in my pocket, together with the passbook which they give me in return for all the rest that I'm leaving behind, and go back to the restaurant. I can't find any food there to my taste.

I'm afraid of not being able to digest it. But already the rumour must have got about that, if I'm not exactly rich, I'm certainly not poor any longer. And, in fact, as I come out of the restaurant, I find a car waiting for me, accompanied by a chauffeur who raises his cap to me with one hand, while with the other he holds the door open for me to get in. I don't know where he takes me. But since I've got a motorcar, it's obvious that, without knowing it, I must have a house. Why yes, a very lovely house. It's an old house, where quite obviously lots of people have lived before me, and lots more will live after me. Is this furniture really mine? I somehow feel myself to be a stranger here, a kind of intruder. Just as this morning at dawn the city seemed deserted, now this house of mine seems deserted. I again feel frightened at hearing the echo of my footsteps, as I move through that immense silence. In winter, evening's soon upon you. I'm cold and I feel tired. I buck up my ideas, however, and start moving about. I open one of the doors, quite at random, and stand there in utter amazement, when I see that the room's ablaze with light. It's the bedroom, and there on the bed . . . There she is! The young woman in the photograph, alive, and with her two bare arms still raised in the air, but this time they're inviting me to hasten over to her so that she may welcome me and joyously clasp me in them.

Is it a dream?

Well, this much is quite certain: just as would happen in a dream, when the night has passed and dawn has ushered in the morning, she's no longer there in that bed. There's no trace of her. And the bed which was so warm during the night, is now, when you touch it, freezing cold, just like a tomb. And the whole house is filled with that smell which lurks in places where dust has settled, where life has been withered away by time. And there's that sensation of irritated tiredness which needs well-regulated and useful habits, simply in order to maintain itself in being. I've always had a horror of them. I want to run away. It's quite impossible that this is my house. This is a nightmare. It's quite obvious that I've dreamt one of the most absurd dreams ever dreamt. And as if seeking proof of this, I go and look at myself in a mirror that's hanging on the wall opposite, and instantly I get the terrible feeling that I'm drowning. I'm terrified, lost in a world of never-ending dismay. From what remote distance are my eyes—those eyes which, so it seems to me, I've had since I was a child—now looking wide-eyed with terror at this old man's face, without being able to convince myself of the truth of what I'm seeing? What, am I old already? So suddenly! Just like that! How is it possible?

I hear a knock at the door. My heart turns over. They tell me my children have arrived.

My *children?*

It seems utterly frightful to me that children should have been born to me. But when? I must have had them yesterday. Yesterday I was still young. It's only right and proper that I should know them, now that I'm old.

They come in, leading several small children by the hand—*their* children. They immediately rush over and tell me to lean on them. Lovingly they reprove me for having got up out of bed. Very solicitously they make me sit down, so that I shan't feel so weary. Me, weary? Why yes, they know perfectly well that I can't stand on my feet any longer and that I'm in a really bad way.

Seated there, I look at them, I listen to them. And I get the feeling that they're playing a joke on me in a dream.

Has my life already come to an end?

And while I sit there looking at them, all bent so solicitously over me, I mischievously observe—almost as if I really ought not to be noticing it—right under my very eyes, I can see, sprouting there on their heads . . . Yes, there's a considerable number of white hairs growing there. Yes, white hair's growing there on their heads.

"There, that proves it's all a joke. *You've* got white hair too."

And look, look at those young people who came through that door just now as tiny children. Look? All they had to do was to come up to my armchair. They've grown up. One of them—yes, that one—is already a charming young lady. She wants the rest of them to make way for her so that she can come and be admired. If her father hadn't grabbed hold of her she'd have thrown herself at me, climbed up on to my knees, put her arm round my neck, and rested her little head on my breast.

I feel the urge to leap to my feet. But I have to admit that I really can't manage it any more. And with the same childlike eyes that a little while before those children had—oh, how grown-up they are now!—I sit there, looking at my old children, standing behind these new ones, and there is great compassion in my gaze.

Isaac Babel

THE SIN OF JESUS

Arina lived by the front staircase where the guests' rooms were. Serioga, the janitor's assistant, lived under the back stairs. Between them, there was shame. On Palm Sunday, Arina presented Serioga with a pair of twins. Water flows, stars shine, people make love. Soon Arina was pregnant again. The sixth month was rolling on— and how they do roll, those women's months!—when Serioga was called in to the Army. There was the snag. So Arina said to him:

"There's no point in my waiting for you, Serioga. We'll be parted for four years and in that time, I'd say, I'll have at least three babies. Working in a hotel, you know, is just like going around with your skirt pulled up. The guest is always the boss, whatever he is, even a Jew. So by the time you get out of the Army, my insides will be pretty worn out and I won't be much of a woman no more, so what's the good?"

"You have something there," Serioga said, nodding.

"Now there are some fellows who'd marry me if I wanted. There's that contractor Trofimych, but he's a brute. And there's Isai Abramych, the warden of St. Nicholas' Church—he's old and weak, but what good does your nasty male vigor do me? I'm sick of it as it is, and that's the truth, I'm telling you, just like I was confessing to a priest. . . . Three months from now, when the baby's born, I'll take it to a foundling home and get hitched to the old fellow."

When he heard that, Serioga removed his belt and bravely whacked Arina a few times on the belly.

"Hey," Arina says to him, "take it easy. It's your stuffing inside this belly, no one else's."

Translated by Andrew R. MacAndrew. From *Lyubka the Cossack and Other Stories* by Isaac Babel, translated by Andrew R. MacAndrew. Copyright © 1963 by Andrew R. MacAndrew. Reprinted by arrangement with The New American Library, Inc., New York.

But there was plenty of beating and pushing and a flood of the man's tears and the woman's blood, but that's not the point. Well, finally the woman came to Jesus Christ and said to Him as follows:

"I," she said, "am Arina, the chambermaid from the Madrid and Louvre Hotel—you know, on Tverskaya Street. As you know, Lord Jesus, working in a hotel is just like going around with your skirt pulled up. Any guy who pays for his room must be treated like your lord and master, even if he's a Jew or something. Now, there walks on earth a servant of yours, Lord Jesus, one Serioga, the janitor's assistant, and last year, on Palm Sunday, I had twins by him. . . ."

And she gave the Lord a complete picture of what had happened.

"But," the Lord asked, "what if Serioga refuses to go into the Army?"

"I guess the cops will come and drag him off."

"Cops?" the Lord said and sadly hung His head. "That's something that hadn't occurred to me. . . . Now, how about your trying to stay chaste for a while?"

"You mean for four years? Listening to you talk one would think it was easy for men to get rid of the beast in them. And even supposing they did, how would they reproduce themselves then? If you want to give me advice, you should talk sense!"

The Lord's cheeks turned red then, for the woman's words had touched Him on a sore spot. But He said nothing. No one can kiss his own ear, and God is aware of that too.

"Now here's what I'll do for you, God's servant, holy sinner, the Lord's handmaiden Arina," the Lord proclaimed in all His glory. "There's a little angel called Alfred hanging around my heaven and lately he's really got out of hand. He whines all the time. 'Why,' he says to me, 'did you have to promote me to Angel when I wasn't even twenty and was still full of sap!' So what would you say, Arina, if I lent you the angel Alfred for four years to serve as a husband? He'd help you pray, he'd protect you, and you could use him as your sweetheart too. As to becoming pregnant by him, you have nothing to fear: you'll never even get a duckling out of him, let alone a child, for while there's a lot of fun in him, there's not even a kopeck's worth of seriousness."

"Now, that's just what I need," the Lord's handmaiden Arina cried happily, "because that seriousness of theirs has made me almost kick the bucket three times in the past two years."

"So you'll have a blissful respite, God's child Arina, and may your prayers be as light as a song. So be it."

And they let it rest at that. Alfred was brought to her and he turned out to be a frail, delicate little guy with a pair of wings behind his bluish shoulders. And those wings seemed to flutter in a sort of rosy light, like a couple of doves playing in the sky at sunset. Arina grabbed him, pressed him in her arms, and sobbed with joy and feminine tenderness.

"Alfred, sweetie-pie, my consolation, my bridegroom . . ."

The Lord warned her though that, before they went to bed, she must remove his wings—they were attached like doors, on sort of hinges—and wrap them carefully in a clean sheet, because any brisk movement could easily snap a wing, which after all, is made only of infants' sighs.

The Lord blessed their union with a specially summoned choir of bishops who performed very loudly indeed. But there were no refreshments, nothing at all—that's strictly against their rules up there. When it was all over, Arina and Alfred, their arms around each other, descended on a silken ladder to earth.

They came to Petrovka Street—the most expensive shopping center, but nothing less would satisfy her now—and she bought for Alfred, who, by the way, was not only sockless but, besides, wore nothing at all and was in what we might call his natural state, patent-leather shoes, checked trousers, a hunting jacket, and a sky-blue velvet waistcoat.

"The rest, darling," she told him, "I'm sure we'll find at home."

Arina managed to get that day off at the hotel. Serioga arrived and started kicking up hell outside her door, but she didn't even go out to him.

"Mr. Nifantich," she told him from behind the closed door, "I happen to be washing my feet today; and therefore I beg you to leave without no more disturbance."

He said nothing and left. It was, of course, the angelic force that was beginning to manifest itself.

That evening, Arina produced a meal good enough for a big merchant, for she had plenty of ambition, that woman. A half bottle of vodka, a bottle of wine, a Danube herring with spuds, and a samovar for tea. No sooner had Alfred partaken of that earthly fruit than he fell dead asleep. So Arina immediately removed his wings from their hinges, packed them up, and carried him to her bed.

And now, on her tattered, sinful comforter, that heavenly wonder was stretched out, with a halo behind his head and light radiating from his body, its rosy beams alternating with the white moonbeams swaying round the room on their luminous legs. Arina cried and laughed and sang and prayed. Ah, Arina, what happiness you've struck on this battered earth! Blessed art thou among women!

They had emptied the half bottle and it showed. As soon as she was asleep, she rolled over, resting her belly, which had been swell-

ing for six months now with Serioga's fruit, on Alfred. It wasn't
enough for her to sleep with an angel, it wasn't enough that no
one spat at the wall or snored or snorted; no, that wasn't enough
for that frantic dame—she had to warm her sore and swollen belly
too. And in her drunken state, she smothered God's angel, smothered him amidst her rejoicing, like one smothers a week-old infant
—crushed him under her weight. And so that was the end of him
and pale tears rolled from his angel's wings wrapped in a sheet.

Dawn came. Trees bowed their heads to the ground; in the distant northern forests, each pine turned into a priest and knelt
down. . . .

And again the woman stood before the Lord's throne. She stood
there, strong and broad-shouldered, holding the young corpse in
her thick, red arms.

"Behold, Lord————"

This time, Jesus' meek heart was unable to stand it and angrily
He laid a curse on the woman.

"From this day on, Arina," the Lord said, "you're on your own.
Let it be with you as it is on earth."

"But why, Lord?" Arina said in a very low voice. "Was it me
myself who made my body so heavy? Was it me who brewed that
vodka? Was it me who made my stupid, lonely soul the way it is?"

"I've had just about as much of you as I can stand," cried the
Lord Jesus. "You've smothered my angel. Ah, you slut————"

And a putrid wind carried Arina back to earth, straight to her
room in the Madrid and Louvre Hotel on Tverskaya Street. And
there, things were as bad as they could be, with Serioga drinking
and running wild, for these were his last days before going into
the army.

And the contractor Trofimych, just back from a trip to Kolomna,
took one look at Arina, sturdy and red-cheeked, and cooed:

"Oh, your cute, fat little tummy," and so on.

Isai Abramych heard about that fat little tummy and he too
came lisping tenderly to her.

"I, of course," he lisped, "cannot make you my lawful wedded
wife after all that's happened. However," he added, "I don't see
why we shouldn't go to bed together now, since . . ."

If that old guy was to lie anywhere, it surely should have been
under a few feet of cold earth rather than in bed with anyone, but
no, he too must have a go at insulting her to her very soul. They
were all after her like dogs who had broken their chains—the
kitchen boys, the traveling salesmen, the foreigners, everyone—
they all wanted to have some fun.

And that's the end of the story.

When she was due to deliver—for three months had rolled by—

Arina stepped out into the courtyard, by the back staircase near the janitor's room, raised her huge belly toward the silky heavens, and made the following stupid statement:

"See, Lord, that's some belly for you! It'd sound like a drum if you dropped peas on it. But I still can't see what it's all about and again, Lord, I never asked for it."

Lord Jesus washed Arina with His tears then, and He, the Saviour, knelt before her.

"Forgive me, Arina dear," He said, "forgive me, your sinful God, for having done this to you. . . ."

"No, there's no forgiveness for you, Lord Jesus," Arina said. "There just ain't."

Pär Lagerkvist

SAVIOUR JOHN

My name is John but I am called the Saviour, because I am to save mankind on earth. I am the one chosen for this and that is why I am so called. I am not like other people; no one here in the town is like me. The Lord has kindled a fire in my breast which never goes out; I can always feel it burning and burning inside, day and night. I feel that I must save them, that I am to be sacrificed for their sake. Through my faith, which I preach to them, they shall be redeemed.

Yes, I feel I must believe—must believe for them. For all who doubt, for all who hunger and thirst and cannot be satisfied. I shall refresh them. In their anguish and need they call to me, and I wipe out everything as with a gentle and merciful hand, and it is no more.

Yes, I am to save mankind on earth. From the age of fourteen I have known that I am chosen for it. Since then I have been different from all others.

I don't dress like other people either—you can tell just from that. I have two rows of silver buttons on my jacket and a green band around my waist, and a red one around my arm. On a string around my neck I wear the lid of a cigar box with the picture of a pretty young woman on it; I can't remember now what it means. That's how I am dressed. But fastened by an invisible thread around my forehead I wear a star which I have cut out of tin. It gleams and sparkles in the sun. It can be seen from afar and it shines so that no one can help noticing it.

Translated by Alan Blair. Original title, "Frälsar-Johan" published in *Onda Sagor* (*Evil Tales*) published by Albert Bonniers Forlag, Stockholm, 1924. Volume included in *The Eternal Smile and Other Stories*, copyright 1954 by Random House, Inc. Reprinted by permission of original publisher. Published in England in *The Marriage Feast and Other Short Stories* and reprinted by permission of Chatto & Windus Ltd.

When I walk down the street everyone stares after me in wonder. Look at the Saviour, they say to each other. For they know that's who I am. They know I have come to save them.

But they don't understand me yet. They don't believe as they should. Not as I believe. There is no fire inside them, not as with me. That is why I must speak to them, teach them to believe; that is why I must stay here for a long time yet.

I think it is so strange—they see their Saviour and hear his voice, he is right among them, and still they do not understand him. But in time to come their eyes will be opened and they will see him as he is.

Market today. Been up to the market place and preached as usual. The farmers were there with their carts. All gathered around me. I spoke of everything that I bear within me, of my message which I shall proclaim to the whole world: that I am come to redeem them, that through me they shall gain peace. They listened attentively; I think they were comforted by my words.

I don't understand why they laugh. I myself never laugh. For me everything is serious. As I stood there looking out over the large crowd of people and thinking that in each one of them there was a soul that must be saved if it was not to go under, that must believe if it was not to plunge into despair, I was moved by such solemnity and earnestness. Oh, it was glorious to stand like that and feel them gathered around me. I seemed for a moment to be looking out over countless multitudes, even all those who had not come to hear me today—for it is quite a small market and there are not so many people; to be looking out over all the people on earth, and all hungered and thirsted for peace, and I was to save them. It was a blissful moment. I shall never forget it.

I think I was filled with the spirit today and that they understood me.

When I had finished, one of them stepped forward and gave me a cabbage on behalf of everyone there. I brought it home and this evening I have made good, nourishing soup from it. It is a long time since I have had anything hot to eat. God bless him.

Oh, the pity of humanity. They are all unhappy, distressed; they all suffer. Johansson, the baker, is unhappy because they no longer buy his bread now that a bakery has opened next door. His bread is so good too; he has often given me a loaf to take home. All bread is good. Ekström, the policeman, whom I often talk to, is unhappy because his wife neglects the house, and I don't think she bothers about him any more. Even the magistrate is unhappy, because he has lost his only son.

Only I am happy. For in me burns the fire of faith which can never go out, which shall burn and burn until it has consumed me. I have no uneasiness, no anxiety; I am not like them. That would not be right.

No, I must not despair. I must believe for them.

They have taken me to the workhouse so that I shall be free of all earthly worries and can devote myself entirely to my mission as Saviour. I am well off here; we get food twice a day. The others here are poor people. I feel so sorry for them. They are quiet, good souls; I don't think anyone has ever understood me so well as they do. They call me the Saviour, like everyone else, and have great respect for me.

In the evenings I preach to them. They listen devoutly, and every word reaches their hearts. How their eyes shine when I speak! They cling to me—to my words—as their only hope. Yes, they know that I have come to save them.

Always after supper I gather them around me like this and speak full of rapture, full of the heavenly light within me; speak of the faith that can overcome everything, that transforms this world to a happy home given us by the Highest. The superintendent says that I may, by all means—it doesn't matter. He is pleased with me. Then we go to rest. There are four of us in our room. The star hangs over my bed; it shines and burns all night long in the dark above me. It casts its light over my face as I sleep. I am not like the others on earth.

Oh, terrifying anguish in my soul! Anguish, despair fills us all.

The star is missing, the star of salvation which alone can guide us aright. This morning when I woke up, the nail I hang it on was empty. No one knows where it has gone. Darkness surrounds us. I look for a single ray of light but find none, no way out of the terrible darkness. All are broken-hearted, the whole town is sunk in grief. From up here at the workhouse we can see it lying like ashes. The sky is gray and leaden, there is no sign of light.

How are we to be saved from our need? How are we to find the way out of the despair that seizes us?

All put their hope in me. But what am I if the star does not shine above my head, if the heavenly light does not lead me? I am nothing then; I am just as poor as all the others.

Who is to save us then?

Now it has been found. All day I have thanked and praised on my knees.

Old Enok had taken it. We found it under his mattress. Now we are all glad and undismayed once more. My faith glows stronger than ever after this trial I have undergone.

He had only done it as a joke. I have forgiven him.

Sometimes I feel such loneliness and emptiness round me. It seems as if people do not understand my message to them. I doubt my power over their souls. How can I redeem them?

They always smile so when I speak. As soon as they see me their faces light up. But do they really believe in me?

I think it is so strange that they do not understand who I am, that they cannot feel the fire which burns inside me—my heavenly rapture—how everything glows and is consumed within me. I can feel it myself so well.

Sometimes when I preach, it is as if I were alone, although there are large crowds listening all around me. I am like a flame leaping higher and higher, rising clearer and purer toward the sky. But no one warms himself at it.

O doubt, that is trying to crush me! What makes us so poor and abased as you do?

Today I have been out with the flowers and the birds. They were so glad because I came. The larks rejoiced; primroses and violets peeped up everywhere out of the grass. I preached for a while in the deepest reverence. Everything listened. The larks stopped above my head to hear me. What peace the soul feels in the country; everything there understands me so well!

If people were flowers and trees, then they would understand me too. Yes, they would be much happier then.

They are bound to the earth and yet do not belong to it. They are flowers plucked up by the roots. The sun only burns them; the soil is just waiting for them to become soil. Nothing here makes them happy; nothing can save them except the message from heaven which I want to bring them. Then everything will be explained and the earth will smell of lilies. Then they will gain peace.

When I came back to the town in the evening, there were a lot of people collected outside the taverns and they called for their Saviour, wanted me to preach to them. But I said that I had been away talking to my God and that I must go home and think over what he had said.

Perhaps that was not right. But I felt like a stranger and went home grieving.

O my heart, how hard it is to live! How heavy to bear is the calling that has been laid upon me!

This afternoon as I walked along the street deep in thought, I found myself in the midst of the children who were coming from school. They flocked around me.

"Look at the Saviour," they cried, "look at the Saviour!" They pressed around from all sides; I had to stop.

Then one of them stretched up his arms and shouted, "Crucified! Crucified!"

I think someone had taught it to them, for with one accord they all did the same.

They stretched up their small hands and all around me their childish voices shouted, "Crucified! Crucified!"

It was as if a sword had pierced my breast. I felt my heart stand still; the sweat of anguish broke out on my brow. With their shouting and noise in my ears I forced my way through them and escaped. I went into the yard of Lundgren, the carpenter, and wept.

I love children. No one loves them as I do. When I look into their bright eyes I feel a joy which nothing else on earth can give. I want them to come to me. Then I would pick them up on my knee and stroke their hair and they would lay their warm little cheeks against mine. . . .

I have often seen Johansson the baker's little boy do that when Johansson has sat down to rest in the evening. I have seen him pat his father's cheek and put his arms around his neck and they have sat like that for a long time without a thought for anything else. It has made me long for a little hand to pat me like that. . . .

But he who is to save mankind walks alone among them like a stranger. He has no home here, no joy, no sorrow that belongs to the earth. He is an outcast, for in him burns the fire that is to consume them. Who is not as they are?

Crucified! Crucified!

Just believe and believe. Believe for them all. Oh, every evening I am as tired as though I had lived their thousand lives. I collapse on my bed and fall asleep like an animal. Only the star burns above my weary body so that I shall waken again and believe still more.

Why have I been chosen for it? Often as I sit at the window up here at the workhouse and look out over the town, I think it is so strange that I of all people shall save them. I am so lowly; many have greater power and might on earth than I. The calling weighs me down like a burden which I am too weak to bear. I want to sink down on my knees. My soul is filled with such anguish. . . .

Their Saviour surely must not sink down. *He* must not feel anguish in his soul.

Oh, why must I, who am weakest of all, believe for them?

This afternoon as I was walking across the market place, I met the magistrate. As he passed he nodded kindly. "Good afternoon, John," he said.

I almost stopped short. . . .

He did not call me the Saviour!

"Good afternoon, John," was all he said. Just John, nothing else.

No one has called me that since I was a child. Now I remember, it was my mother who called me that. She would pick me up on her knee and stroke my head. I remember it so well now that I think back. . . .

Good afternoon, John. . . .

She was so good to me. In the evenings she would come home and light the lamp and prepare the food, and then I would creep up on her knee. Her hair was quite golden, her hands nice and white from scrubbing floors all day. Now I remember it all so well—it is her I carry around my neck, it is Mother.

Good afternoon, John. . . .

How nice it felt when he said that. So nice and safe. All seemed to grow quite still inside me, no worry, no fear of anything. Just John, nothing else.

Oh, if only I could be like all the others! If I could take off the sign of my Saviour's calling and go about like one of them; just be as they are. Live here quietly and peacefully with my earthly work, as the others do, day after day; and in the evening go to bed tired from worldly tasks, which I have done as I should, not from believing, just believing . . .

Perhaps I could be a turner at Lundgren the carpenter's. Or, if that was difficult, then I could sweep the yard.

And so I would be like them. And there would not be this fire burning in me any more! No anguish would consume me any more.

Just John, nothing else . . . They would all know so well who I was, would see me every day going about my business. John, he's the one who sweeps the yard. . . .

Oh, why must I save them, I who am the poorest and weakest of all? I who want to live here in peace, so grateful for the earth which has bidden me here to it. Like a guest, sunk down on his knees at the rich table; like a flower that scarcely raises itself above the ground.

O God, my Father, if it be possible, then let this cup pass from me!

No, no! I must not doubt! Not fail them!

What is it that wants to lead my soul astray? What is it that wants to hurl them all down into an abyss of darkness, because I fail them?

Something terrible has happened to me! What is it? Do I not believe any more?

Yes, yes! I believe! I believe as never before. I shall save them. It is *I*, it is *I* who will save them.

I walk and walk here at night, have no peace. In the streets, out on the roads, far into the woods and back again. There is a wind, the clouds are driving before it. Where am I—my head is burning —I am so tired. . . .

Yes, I believe! I believe! I shall save them, I shall be sacrificed for them. Soon, soon . . .

Why, then, do I feel such anguish? Surely the Saviour of mankind must not fear and despair as I do?

No, no . . .

Am I out in the woods again? Don't I hear the trees soughing? Why am I wandering about here? Why am I not with the people who are waiting and waiting? . . .

But they don't understand me!

How are they to understand me when I am nothing but despair and torment? How are they to believe in me when I wander about in the darkness without peace?

I cannot save them! It is not I, not I!

Yes, their Saviour is all the anguish and need that they do not understand. He is like a bird crying in the sky far above their heads. They hear his cries up there but think it is not for them, because he is floating so high. Not until he falls dead and bleeding to earth do they understand him. Only then can they believe.

Crucified! Crucified!

Yes, I want to be sacrificed, I want to be sacrificed!

They shall be redeemed by my blood, by my poor blood. Soon, soon it will happen. . . .

Sleep sweetly all small flowers here in the darkness, all meadows, all trees, all people in the world. Have peace, dear earth. I shall redeem you.

I watch over you in the night. All your anguish is mine. You shall not suffer, not be troubled about anything. I shall lay down my life for you.

How silent it is here in the wood! Am I walking on dead leaves? My footsteps make no sound.

Many flowers and leaves are moldering now in the autumn and it is so soft under the trees, silent and soft. There is a smell of earth.

Is that the clock striking in the town? One—two—

Oh, I am so tired, so tired—I want to go home.

I must go home now and rest, lie down for a while. They will be wondering where I am.

I must be coming out onto the road now. It is muddy—I think it rained yesterday—how windy it is!

No, it is the bell ringing and ringing! It booms in the air. What is it? It sounds terrible. There are a lot of them, they are tolling and booming as though for Judgment Day! What is it? I must run!

Fire! Fire! The flames are leaping up, the sky is blood red! The town is on fire! The world is on fire, it is perishing!

O God, I must save them! I must save them. They are waiting for me—isn't he coming, isn't he coming. . . .

Yes, I'm running, I'm running. I am coming to save them. It's the mud clinging to me. I'm running!

Heaven and earth are on fire! They are crashing down. Like a sea of fire. I must save them, I must save them!

My heart, you must not pain me—good heart, don't pain me so, I cannot run then, cannot breathe—and I must save them! You know that I must save them.

Nothing but a blazing sea! And the storm rages. Heaven is driving in flames across the world and setting it alight.

Now, now the others are beside me. They are running in the same direction as I.

"The world is perishing," I shout at them.

"Oh," they reply, "it's only the workhouse."

Yes, it's the workhouse! All those poor people, those who hunger and thirst because they cannot believe, they're burning to death! They are perishing! Only I can save them!

My heart, do not hurt so; we are nearly there—soon, soon . . .

The flames leap up, the smoke is here in the street, I can feel the heat. . . .

Now I am there.

The superintendent—a lot of people have collected here.

"I shall save them, I shall save them!" I shout.

"There's no one there to save!" they call, placing themselves in the way. They don't understand me. I rush into the flames.

The heat almost stuns me. No, I do not sink down—their Saviour must not sink down. I only stagger at first—grope my way forward—through the hall—into the rooms. . . .

It is empty here—they are upstairs. . . .

The smoke nearly stifles me on the stairs. No, no, I do not sink down. I shall save them—all—all. . . .

Where are they?

I grope my way forward in a daze. The smoke is thick—the flames leap up—I lurch about. . . .

Where are they?

Old Man Enok who cannot manage by himself—and Anton whose legs are paralyzed—and old Kristina who is out of her wits—and Samuelsson—and Manfred from the jail . . .

I can't find them. . . .

I creep along the floor. The flames lick after me. There is a crackling all around me—a roar—it's collapsing. . . . Where are they? They have moved the furniture out, the beds, the chairs. . . . It's bare and empty—as though nobody lived here. Where are they? They can't be here—only I—only I. . . .

It's on fire! On fire! The beams crash down. The flames leap up everywhere. I rush around. Where are they—where are they? All the poor—I can't find them—they're not here. . . . Only fire and devastation—only I—only I . . .

O my heart, is it you that is burning? Perhaps it's only you. I can feel you consuming my body, my breast, my limbs, until nothing is left but you! Yes, consume it, consume it! I want only to be you, only you, heart that hungers and thirsts, only you, fire that devours me!

Nothing else—nothing else—only you . . .

No—I can't go on any—any longer. . . . It's the end. . . . Yes, yes, I sink down—it's the end—end. . . .

O God, forgive me for not finding the people I was to save. I can't find them. Forgive a heart that's on fire—only with longing to be sacrificed—to die—to die. . . .

Yes, I feel that you forgive me. You forgive the heart that burns for you—you love it—yes, you love it. You let it be consumed—consumed—you let it have peace—peace. . . .

Crucified! Crucified!

Heinrich Böll

MY MELANCHOLY FACE

As I stood by the harbor to watch the gulls, my melancholy face attracted a policeman who walked the beat in this quarter. I was completely absorbed in the sight of the floating birds, who shot up and plunged down, looking in vain for something edible: the harbor was desolate, the water greenish, thick with dirty oil, and in its crusted skin floated all kinds of discarded rubbish. Not a ship was to be seen, the cranes were rusty, the warehouses decayed; it seemed that not even rats populated the black debris on the quai; it was quiet. For many years all connections with the outside had been cut off.

I had fixed my eyes on one particular gull whose flight I was watching. It hovered near the surface of the water, nervous as a swallow that senses the approach of a thunderstorm; only once in a while did it dare the screeching leap upward to unite its course with that of its companions. If I could have made one wish, I would have chosen bread to feed it to the gulls, to break crumbs and fix a white point for the purposeless wings, to set a goal toward which they would fly; to tighten this shrieking web of chaotic trails by a toss of a bread crumb, grasping into them as into a pile of strings that one gathers up. But like them, I too was hungry; tired too, yet happy in spite of my melancholy because it was good to stand there, hands in my pockets, and watch the gulls and drink sadness.

But suddenly an official hand was laid on my shoulder, and a voice said: "Come along!" With this, the hand tried to jerk me around by the shoulder. I stood where I was, shook it off, and said calmly: "You're crazy."

Translated by Rainer Schulte and Sandra Smith from *Wo Warst Du, Adam? Und Erzählungen,* by Heinrich Böll, published by Friedrich Middelhauve Verlag, Köln, 1967.

"Comrade," the still invisible person said to me, "I'm warning you."

"My dear sir," I replied.

"There are no 'sirs'," he cried angrily. "We're all comrades!" And now he stepped up beside me, looked at me from the side, and I was forced to pull back my happily roaming gaze and sink it into his good eyes: he was serious as a buffalo who has eaten nothing but duty for decades.

"What grounds . . .," I tried to begin . . .

"Grounds enough," he said, "your melancholy face."

I laughed.

"Don't laugh!" His anger was genuine. At first I had thought he was bored, because there were no unregistered whores, no staggering sailors, no thieves or absconders to arrest, but now I saw that it was serious: he wanted to arrest me.

"Come along . . . !"

"And why?" I asked calmly.

Before I became aware of it, my left wrist was enclosed in a thin chain, and at this moment I realized that I was lost again. One last time I turned to the roving gulls, glanced into the beautiful gray sky, and tried, with a sudden twist, to throw myself into the water, for it seemed better to me, after all, to drown alone in this filthy water than to be strangled in some backyard by the myrmidons or be locked up again. But the policeman, with a jerk, drew me so close that escape was no longer possible.

"And why?" I asked again.

"There's a law that you have to be happy."

"I am happy," I cried.

"Your melancholy face . . .," he shook his head.

"But this law is new," I said.

"It's thirty-six hours old, and you know very well that every new law goes into effect twenty-four hours after its proclamation."

"But I don't know it."

"That's no excuse. It was announced day before yesterday, over all the loudspeakers, in all the papers, and it was published in handbills to those," here he looked at me scornfully, "those who have no access to the blessings of the press or the radio; they were scattered over every street in the area. So we'll see where you've spent the last thirty-six hours, comrade."

He dragged me on. Only now did I feel that it was cold and I had no coat, only now did my hunger assert itself and growl before the gates of my stomach, only now did I realize that I was also dirty, unshaven, ragged, and that there were laws that said every comrade was obliged to be clean, shaved, happy, and well-fed. He shoved me in front of him like a scarecrow who, convicted of stealing, had to leave the home of its dreams on the edge of the field. The streets were empty, the way to the precinct not long, and although I had known they would find some reason to arrest me again, still my heart grew heavy, because he led me through the places of my youth, which I had wanted to visit after viewing the harbor: gardens that had been full of shrubs, lovely in their disorder, overgrown paths—all this was now planned, ordered, neat, laid out in squares for the patriotic leagues which had to carry out their exercises here Mondays, Wednesdays, and Saturdays. Only the sky had its former shape and the air was like in those days when my heart had been full of dreams.

Here and there in passing I saw that already in many of the love barracks the state sign had been hung out for those whose turn to participate in the hygienic pleasure was on Wednesday; also many bars seemed authorized to display the sign of drinking, a beer glass stamped out of lead with stripes of the patriotic colors of the area: light-brown, dark-brown, light-brown. No doubt joy reigned already in the hearts of those who had been entered in the state lists of Wednesday drinkers, and could partake of a Wednesday beer.

The unmistakable sign of zeal adhered to everyone who met us, the thin aura of industry surrounded them, probably all the more when they caught sight of the policeman; they all walked faster, showed a perfectly dutiful face, and the women who came out of the stores tried to give their faces an expression of that joy which was expected from them, for they were commanded to show joy, vigorous cheerfulness about the duties of the housewife, who was encouraged to refresh the public worker with a good meal in the evening.

But all these people avoided us skillfully, so that no one had to cross our path directly; wherever signs of life were evident on the street, they disappeared twenty steps ahead of us. Everyone tried to step quickly into a store or turn a corner, and many may have entered an unfamiliar house and waited uneasily behind the door until our steps had faded away.

Only once, just as we were passing a crossing, an older man met us; briefly, I recognized the badge of the schoolteacher on him; it was too late for him to dodge us, and he now tried, after he had first greeted the policeman according to the prescribed regulations (that is, he hit himself three times on the head with a flat hand as a sign of absolute humility), then he tried to fulfill his duty, which demanded that he spit in my face three times and call me the obligatory name: "Traitorous swine." He aimed well, but the day had been hot, his throat must have been dry, because only a few meager, rather unsubstantial drops hit me—which I— against regulations—automatically tried to wipe off with my sleeve; whereupon the policeman kicked me in the behind and hit me with his fist in the middle of my backbone, adding in a calm voice: "Stage 1," which meant the first, mildest form of punishment every policeman could use.

The schoolteacher hurried away quickly. Otherwise everyone succeeded in avoiding us; only one woman, a pale, puffy blonde, taking her prescribed airing beside a love barrack before the evening pleasure, quickly threw me a kiss and I smiled gratefully, while the policeman tried to act as though he hadn't noticed anything. They are urged to allow these women freedoms that would immediately bring any other comrade a heavy punishment. Since they contribute substantially to the improvement of general working morale, they are thought of as standing outside the law, a concession whose significance the state philosopher Dr. Dr. Dr. Bleigoeth branded in the obligatory Journal of (State) Philosophy as a sign of beginning liberalization. I had read it the day before on my way to the capital, when I found a few pages of the magazine in the outhouse of a farm. A student—probably the farmer's son—had glossed it with astute comments.

Luckily we were about to reach the police station, when the sirens started to sound, which meant that the streets would overflow with thousands of people whose faces bore an expression of mild joy (for it was "recommended" not to show too great a joy after work since it would indicate that work was a burden; jubilation, however, was to reign at the beginning of work, jubilation and song)—all these thousands of people would have had to spit at me. Actually the sirens indicated that it was ten minutes before closing, for everyone was expected to indulge in a thorough washing for ten minutes, in accordance with the slogan of the present Chief of State: Happiness and Soap.

At the door to the precinct of this quarter, a plain concrete structure, two guards were posted who bestowed upon me in passing the usual "physical measures": they hit me violently on the temples with their bayonets and cracked the barrels of their pistols against my collarbone, following the preamble to State Law No. 1: "Every policeman except the arresting officer is to prove himself before every apprehended (they mean arrested) as an individual power; to the arresting officer falls the good fortune of executing all necessary bodily measures during the interrogation." The State Law No. 1 itself has the following wording: "Every policeman *may* punish anyone; he *must* punish everyone who has been found guilty of a transgression. There is, for all comrades, no exemption from punishment, but a possibility of exemption from punishment."

We now walked through a long, bare corridor, with many large windows; then a door opened automatically, because in the meantime the guards had announced our arrival, since in those days when everyone was happy, good, orderly, and everyone exerted himself to consume the prescribed pound of soap a day, in those days the arrival of an apprehended (an arrested) was indeed an event.

We entered an almost empty room, which contained only a desk with a telephone and two chairs; I was to place myself in the middle of the room; the policeman took off his helmet and sat down.

At first it was silent and nothing happened; they always do it that way; that's the worst part; I felt how my face sagged more and more, I was hungry and tired, and even the last trace of that joy of melancholy had vanished, for I knew that I was lost.

After a few seconds a tall, pale man entered in the brownish uniform of the pre-examiner; he sat down without saying a word and looked at me.

"Occupation?"

"Simple Comrade."

"Born?"

"1.1 one," I said.

"Last employment?"

"Prisoner."

The two looked at each other.

"When and where released?"

"Yesterday, house 12, cell 13."

"Released to where?"

"To the capital."

"Papers."

I took my release paper out of my pocket and handed it over. He fastened it to the green card on which he had started to write my statements.

"Former offense?"

"Happy face."

The two looked at each other.

"Explain," said the pre-examiner.

"At that time," I said, "my happy face attracted a policeman on a day when general mourning was ordered. It was the anniversary of the death of the chief."

"Length of punishment?"

"Five."

"Conduct?"

"Bad."

"Reason?"

"Lack of initiative."

"That's all."

Then the pre-examiner stood up, walked up to me and knocked out exactly three front middle teeth: a sign that I should be branded as a backslider, a measure I had not reckoned with. Then the pre-examiner left the room and a heavy fellow in a dark brown uniform stepped in: the Interrogator.

They all beat me: the Interrogator, the Senior Interrogator, the Head Interrogator, the Preliminary and Final Judge, and also the policeman carried out all the physical measures, as the law commanded; and they sentenced me to ten years because of my melancholy face, just as five years ago they had sentenced me to five years because of my happy face.

But I must try to have no face at all any more, if I succeed in enduring the next ten years with happiness and soap.

Gottfried Benn

BRAINS

He who believes that one can lie
with words might think that it
was happening here.

Rönne, a young doctor who previously dissected a great deal, was traveling north through southern Germany. The last months he spent doing nothing; for two years he had been employed at a pathological institute: two thousand corpses had passed unconsciously through his hands. This had exhausted him in a peculiar and obscure manner.

Sitting in a corner seat he was watching the passing landscape. He said to himself: we are traveling through wine country, quite flat, past scarlet fields smoking with poppies. It is not too hot. A damp blue, wafted up from shores, floods the sky. Every house leans on roses; some are completely engulfed. I am going to buy myself a notebook and pencil and write down as much as I can so everything won't flow away. I have lived so many years and everything has drowned. Did it stay with me at the beginning? I don't know any more.

In many tunnels eyes lay in wait for light. Men pitching hay; wood and stone bridges; a town, a car on a hill driving up to a house.

On the top of a mountain he saw halls, verandas, and sheds through the woods; there Rönne would replace the head physician for a few weeks. Life is so strong, he thought. This hand will not undermine it, and he looked at his right hand.

On the grounds no one but employees and patients; the sana-

Translated by Rainer Schulte from *Gesammelte Werke* by Gottfried Benn in 4 vols., edited by Dieter Wellershoff. Vol. 2, *Prosa und Szenen*, Limes Verlag, Wiesbaden, 1965.

torium lay quite high; Rönne felt solemn; bathed in the aura of his loneliness, he discussed official matters detachedly with the nurses.

He left everything to them; turning the levers, fastening the lamps, starting the motors, illuminating this and that with a mirror—it pleased him to see science reduced to a series of manual gestures, the coarser ones worthy of a smith, the finer ones of a watchmaker. Then he passed his hands over the X-ray tube, moved the quicksilver of the quartz lamp, widened or narrowed a slit through which light fell on a back, pushed a funnel into an ear, placed cotton in the auditory canal, and examined the effects of these procedures on the patient: how ideas were formed of helper, cure, good doctor, of general trust and joy, and how the removal of fluids merged into the realm of the spiritual. Then an emergency case: he took a wooden splint padded with cotton to place it under the injured finger and wrapped a bandage around it. He wondered whether a leap over a ditch or an overlooked root, arrogance or carelessness had caused it, and how deeply the broken finger was connected with the course and fate of this life, now that he had to attend to it like a distant and escaped person. The moment the pain set in he heard a more distant voice echoing from the depths.

It was customary in the hospital, for death is bureaucratic and dirty, to release hopeless cases to their families, concealing the facts. Rönne walked up to such a case, looked at him: the artificial opening in the front, the back raw with bed sores, and in between some soft flesh; he congratulated him on the successful cure and watched him as he trotted away. Now he'll go home and consider the pains a burdensome symptom of the convalescence, thought Rönne, and under the illusion of renewal admonish his son, instruct his daughter, respect his fellow citizen, and accept his neighbor's prejudices—until the night comes with the blood in his throat. He who believes that one can lie with words might think that it was happening here. But if I could lie with words, I probably wouldn't be here. Wherever I look, a word is needed to live. If I had only lied when I said to him: Good luck!

Shaken, Rönne sat one morning at his breakfast table, deeply depressed: the chief physician would go away on a trip, a replacement would come, get out of bed at this hour and eat the roll: you think you are eating the breakfast but the breakfast is eating you. Nevertheless he went on taking care of the necessary questions and requisitions at the hospital; he tapped with a finger of the right hand on one of the left, a lung emerged. He walked up to beds: good morning, how is your stomach? However, it happened now and then that he walked through the wards without duly questioning each patient about the number of his coughing fits or the temperature of his bowels. When I walk through the wards—

this bothered him a great deal—I fall into every two eyes, am perceived and judged. I am connected with friendly and serious subjects; perhaps I am received in a house in which they long to be, perhaps as a piece of oak-bark which they once tasted. I also had two eyes once whose gaze went backward; yes, indeed I was present: unquestioning and collected. Where have I come to? Where am I? A small fluttering, a breeze.

He thought about its beginning, but didn't know any more: I walk through a street, see a house, and I am reminded of a castle in Florence; they exist together only for a flash, and fade.

Something is weakening me from above. I have no more focus behind my eyes. Space sways so endlessly; once it did flow in one place. The rind that once carried me has decayed.

Often when he returned from such rounds to his room, he turned his hands back and forth and looked at them. Once a nurse observed how he smelled them, or rather how he passed over them as if he were testing their air, how he cupped them, and then moved them as if he were breaking a large soft fruit or bending something apart. She mentioned the incident to the other nurses, but no one could interpret it. Until one day at the hospital a rather large animal was butchered. Rönne came by, apparently by accident, as the head was split open; he took the head in his hands and broke the two halves apart. It occurred to the nurse that this was the movement she had observed in the corridor. But she could not relate this incident to the other and soon forgot it.

Rönne however walked through the gardens. It was summer: adders' tongues rocked the blue of the sky, and roses bloomed sweetheaded. He sensed the power of the earth: up to his soles, and the swell of the forces: no longer through his blood. Primarily, he took shaded paths and those with many benches; frequently he had to rest because of the vehemence of the light, and he felt himself abandoned to a breathless sky.

Gradually he began to attend to his duty only sporadically. He literally fell apart when called upon by the superintendent or the matron to express an opinion on any given matter, when he felt it was important to say something about the subject in question. What should be said about the incident? If it didn't happen this way, it would happen differently. The place would not stay empty. He only wanted to relax in his room and stare at the floor.

When he was lying down, he did not lie like one who had arrived there only a few weeks ago, from a lake over the mountains, but rather as if he had grown up with the place where his body now lay, and had been weakened by the long years; and something stiff and waxy was on him for a long time, as if taken from the bodies he touched.

In the time that followed he busied himself a good deal with his hands. The nurse who waited on him liked him very much: he always spoke so pleadingly with her, although she didn't know why. Often he began contemptuously: he knew these strange formations, his hands had held them. But immediately he lapsed again: they lived by laws which are not made by us, and their fate is as foreign to us as that of a river on which we travel. Then totally extinguished, his gaze already in darkness—it is a matter of twelve chemical elements which came together, not at his bidding, and would separate without asking him. Why should one say anything? There is only air blowing across them.

Disassociated from everything, he had no more power over space, he once said; he barely stirred and lay there almost constantly.

He locked his room after him, so that no one could burst in; he wanted to open the door with self-control.

He arranged for the hospital cars to travel back and forth on the road; it soothed him to hear the noise of cars: distant remembrances in a strange city.

He always lay in one position: stiff on his back. He lay on his back in a long chair, the chair in a square room, the room in a house, and the house on a hill. Except for a few birds he was the highest animal. Thus the earth carried him softly through the ether and, without jarring him, past all the stars.

One night he went to the wards. Along the rows of chaises the patients quietly awaited recovery under their blankets. He looked at them as they lay there; all in homes between happiness and death, in sleep full of dreams about return at evening, of songs from father to son. He looked up and down the ward and went back to his room.

The head physician was called back. He was a friendly man. One of his daughters had fallen ill. Rönne said: Do you see, in these, my hands, I held them, a hundred or even a thousand of them; some were hard, some were soft, all were very fluid; men, women, pulpy and full of blood. Now I hold my own in my hands and wonder what could have happened if at birth the forceps had pressed a bit harder here on the temple . . .? What if someone had continually hit me on a certain spot of the head . . .? What is there about brains? I always wanted to soar upward, like a bird out of a chasm; now I live outside in crystal. Please clear the way, I am floating again—I was so tired—on wings I shall fly—with my sword of blue anemones—in a burst of light at high noon—in ruins of the South—in breaking clouds—atomization of the brow—decomposition of the temple.

Jorge Luis Borges

FUNES THE MEMORIOUS

I remember him (I have no right to utter this sacred verb, only one man on earth had that right and he is dead) with a dark passion flower in his hand, seeing it as no one has ever seen it, though he might look at it from the twilight of dawn till that of evening, a whole lifetime. I remember him, with his face taciturn and Indian-like and singularly *remote*, behind the cigarette. I remember (I think) his angular, leather-braiding hands. I remember near those hands a maté gourd bearing the Uruguayan coat of arms; I remember a yellow screen with a vague lake landscape in the window of his house. I clearly remember his voice: the slow, resentful, nasal voice of the old-time dweller of the suburbs, without the Italian sibilants we have today. I never saw him more than three times; the last was in 1887 . . . I find it very satisfactory that all those who knew him should write about him; my testimony will perhaps be the shortest and no doubt the poorest, but not the most impartial in the volume you will edit. My deplorable status as an Argentine will prevent me from indulging in a dithyramb, an obligatory genre in Uruguay whenever the subject is an Uruguayan. *Highbrow, city slicker, dude*: Funes never spoke these injurious words, but I am sufficiently certain I represented for him those misfortunes. Pedro Leandro Ipuche has written that Funes was a precursor of the supermen, "a vernacular and rustic Zarathustra"; I shall not debate the point, but one should not forget that he was also a kid from Fray Bentos, with certain incurable limitations.

My first memory of Funes is very perspicuous. I can see him on an afternoon in March or February of the year 1884. My father, that year, had taken me to spend the summer in Fray Bentos. I was returning from the San Francisco ranch with my cousin Bernardo Haedo. We were singing as we rode along and being on horseback was not the only circumstance determining my happiness. After a sultry day, an enormous slate-colored storm had hidden the sky. It was urged on by a southern wind, the trees were already going wild; I was afraid (I was hopeful) that the elemental rain would take us by surprise in the open. We were running a kind of race with the storm. We entered an alleyway that sank down between two very high brick sidewalks. It had suddenly got dark; I heard some rapid and almost secret footsteps up above; I raised my eyes and saw a boy running along the narrow and broken path as if it were a narrow and broken wall. I remember his baggy gaucho trousers, his rope-soled shoes, I remember the cigarette in his hard face, against the now limitless storm cloud. Bernardo cried to him unexpectedly: "What time is it, Ireneo?" Without consulting the sky, without stopping, he replied: "It's four minutes to eight, young Bernardo Juan Francisco." His voice was shrill, mocking.

I am so unperceptive that the dialogue I have just related would not have attracted my attention had it not been stressed by my cousin, who (I believe) was prompted by a certain local pride and the desire to show that he was indifferent to the other's tripartite reply.

He told me the fellow in the alleyway was one Ireneo Funes, known for certain peculiarities such as avoiding contact with people and always knowing what time it was, like a clock. He added that he was the son of the ironing woman in town, María Clementina Funes, and that some people said his father was a doctor at the meat packers, an Englishman by the name of O'Connor, and others that he was a horse tamer or scout from the Salto district. He lived with his mother, around the corner from the Laureles house.

During the years eighty-five and eighty-six we spent the summer in Montevideo. In eighty-seven I returned to Fray Bentos. I asked, as was natural, about all my acquaintances and, finally, about the "chronometrical" Funes. I was told he had been thrown by a half-tamed horse on the San Francisco ranch and was left hopelessly paralyzed. I remember the sensation of uneasy magic the news produced in me: the only time I had seen him, we were returning from San Francisco on horseback and he was running along a high place; this fact, told me by my cousin Bernardo, had much of the quality of a dream made up of previous elements. I was told he never moved from his cot, with his eyes fixed on the fig tree in the back or on a spider web. In the afternoons, he would let himself be brought out to the window. He carried his pride to the point of acting as if the blow that had felled him were beneficial . . . Twice I saw him behind the iron grating of the window, which harshly emphasized his condition as a perpetual prisoner: once, motionless, with his eyes closed; another time, again motionless, absorbed in the contemplation of a fragrant sprig of santonica.

Not without a certain vaingloriousness, I had begun at that time my methodical study of Latin. My valise contained the *De viris illustribus* of Lhomond, Quicherat's *Thesaurus*, the commentaries of Julius Caesar and an odd volume of Pliny's *Naturalis historia*, which then exceeded (and still exceeds) my moderate virtues as a Latinist. Everything becomes public in a small town; Ireneo, in his house on the outskirts, did not take long to learn of the arrival of these anomalous books. He sent me a flowery and ceremonious letter in which he recalled our encounter, unfortunately brief, "on the seventh day of February of the year 1884," praised the glorious services my uncle Gregorio Haedo, deceased that same year, "had rendered to our two nations in the valiant battle of Ituzaingó" and requested the loan of any one of my volumes, accompanied by a dictionary "for the proper intelligence of the original text, for I am as yet ignorant of Latin." He promised to return them to me in good condition, almost immediately. His handwriting was perfect, very sharply outlined; his orthography, of the type favored by Andrés Bello: *i* for *y*, *j* for *g*. At first I naturally feared a joke. My cousins assured me that was not the case, that these were peculiarities of Ireneo. I did not know whether to attribute to insolence, ignorance or stupidity the idea that the arduous Latin tongue should require no other instrument than a dictionary; to disillusion him fully, I sent him the *Gradus ad Parnassum* of Quicherat and the work by Pliny.

On the fourteenth of February, I received a telegram from Buenos Aires saying I should return immediately, because my father was "not at all well." May God forgive me; the prestige of being the recipient of an urgent telegram, the desire to communicate to all Fray Bentos the contradiction between the negative form of the message and the peremptory adverb, the temptation to dramatize my suffering, affecting a virile stoicism, perhaps distracted me from all possibility of real sorrow. When I packed my valise, I noticed the *Gradus* and the first volume of the *Naturalis historia* were missing. The *Saturn* was sailing the next day, in the morning; that night, after supper, I headed toward Funes' house. I was astonished to find the evening no less oppressive than the day had been.

At the respectable little house, Funes' mother opened the door for me.

She told me Ireneo was in the back room and I should not be surprised to find him in the dark, because he knew how to pass the idle hours without lighting the candle. I crossed the tile patio, the little passageway; I reached the second patio. There was a grape arbor; the darkness seemed complete to me. I suddenly heard Ireneo's high-pitched, mocking voice. His voice was speaking in Latin; his voice (which came from the darkness) was articulating with morose delight a speech or prayer or incantation. The Roman syllables resounded in the earthen patio; my fear took them to be indecipherable, interminable; afterward, in the enormous dialogue of that night, I learned they formed the first paragraph of the twenty-fourth chapter of the seventh book of the *Naturalis historia*. The subject of that chapter is memory; the last words were *ut nihil non iisdem verbis redderetur auditum*.

Without the slightest change of voice, Ireneo told me to come in. He was on his cot, smoking. It seems to me I did not see his face until dawn; I believe I recall the intermittent glow of his cigarette. The room smelled vaguely of dampness. I sat down; I repeated the story about the telegram and my father's illness.

I now arrive at the most difficult point in my story. This story (it is well the reader know it by now) has no other plot than that dialogue which took place half a century ago. I shall not try to reproduce the words, which are now irrecoverable. I prefer to summarize with veracity the many things Ireneo told me. The indirect style is remote and weak; I know I am sacrificing the efficacy of my narrative; my readers should imagine for themselves the hesitant periods which overwhelmed me that night.

Ireneo began by enumerating, in Latin and in Spanish, the cases of prodigious memory recorded in the *Naturalis historia*: Cyrus, king of the Persians, who could call every soldier in his armies by name, Mithridates Eupator, who administered the law in the twenty-two languages of his empire; Simonides, inventor of the science of mnemonics; Metrodorus, who practiced the art of faithfully repeating what he had heard only once. In obvious good faith, Ireneo was amazed that such cases be considered amazing. He told me that before that rainy afternoon when the blue-gray horse threw him, he had been what all humans are: blind, deaf, addlebrained, absent-minded. (I tried to remind him of his exact perception of time, his memory for proper names; he paid no attention to me.) For nineteen years he had lived as one in a dream: he looked without seeing, listened without hearing, forgetting everything, almost everything. When he fell, he became unconscious; when he came to, the present was almost intolerable in its richness and sharpness, as were his most distant and trivial memories. Somewhat later he learned that he was paralyzed. The fact scarcely interested him. He reasoned (he felt) that his immobility was a minimum price to pay. Now his perception and his memory were infallible.

We, at one glance, can perceive three glasses on a table; Funes, all the leaves and tendrils and fruit that make up a grape vine. He knew by heart the forms of the southern clouds at dawn on the 30th of April, 1882, and could compare them in his memory with the mottled streaks on a book in Spanish binding he had only seen once and with the outlines of the foam raised by an oar in the Río Negro the night before the Quebracho uprising. These memories were not simple ones; each visual image was linked to muscular sensations, thermal sensations, etc. He could reconstruct all his dreams, all his half-dreams. Two or three times he had reconstructed a whole day; he never hesitated, but each reconstruction had required a whole day. He told me: "I alone have more memories than all mankind has probably had since the world has been the world." And again: "My dreams are like you people's waking hours." And again, toward dawn: "My memory, sir, is like a garbage heap." A circle drawn on a blackboard, a right triangle, a lozenge—all these are forms we can fully and intuitively grasp; Ireneo could do the same with the stormy mane of a pony, with a herd of cattle on a hill, with the changing fire and its innumerable ashes, with the many faces of a dead man throughout a long wake. I don't know how many stars he could see in the sky.

These things he told me; neither then nor later have I ever placed them in doubt. In those days there were no cinemas or phonographs; nevertheless, it is odd and even incredible that no one ever performed an experiment with Funes. The truth is that we live out our lives putting off all that can be put off; perhaps we all know deep down that we are immortal and that sooner or later all men will do and know all things.

Out of the darkness, Funes' voice went on talking to me.

He told me that in 1886 he had invented an original system of numbering and that in a very few days he had gone beyond the twenty-four-thousand mark. He had not written it down, since anything he thought of once would never be lost to him. His first stimulus was, I think, his discomfort at the fact that the famous thirty-three gauchos of Uruguayan history should require two signs and two words, in place of a single word and a single sign. He then applied this absurd principle to the other numbers. In place of seven thousand thirteen, he would say (for example) *Máximo Pérez*; in place of seven thousand fourteen, *The Railroad*; other numbers were *Luis Melián Lafinur, Olimar, sulphur, the reins, the whale, the gas, the caldron, Napoleon, Agustín de Vedia*. In place of five hundred, he would say *nine*. Each word had a particular sign, a kind of mark; the last in the series were very complicated . . . I tried to explain to him that this rhapsody of incoherent terms was precisely the opposite of a system of numbers. I told him that saying 365 meant saying three hundreds, six tens, five ones, an analysis which is not found in the "numbers" *The Negro Timoteo* or *meat blanket*. Funes did not understand me or refused to understand me.

Locke, in the seventeenth century, postulated (and rejected) an impossible language in which each individual thing, each stone, each bird and each branch, would have its own name; Funes once projected an analogous language, but discarded it because it seemed too general to him, too ambiguous. In fact, Funes remembered not only every leaf of every tree of every wood, but also every one of the times he had perceived or imagined it. He decided to reduce each of his past days to some seventy thousand memories, which would then be defined by means of ciphers. He was dissuaded from this by two considerations: his awareness that the task was interminable, his awareness that it was useless. He thought that by the hour of his death he would not even have finished classifying all the memories of his childhood.

The two projects I have indicated (an infinite vocabulary for the natural series of numbers, a useless mental catalogue of all the images of his memory) are senseless, but they betray a certain stammering grandeur. They permit us to glimpse or infer the nature of Funes' vertiginous world. He was, let us not forget, almost incapable of ideas of a general, Platonic sort. Not only was it difficult for him to comprehend that the generic symbol *dog* embraces so many unlike individuals of diverse size and form; it bothered him that the dog at three fourteen (seen from the side) should have the same name as the dog at three fifteen (seen from the front). His own face in the mirror, his own hands, surprised him every time he saw them. Swift relates that the emperor of Lilliput could discern the movement of the minute hand; Funes could continuously discern the tranquil advances of corruption, of decay, of fatigue. He could note the progress of death, of dampness. He was the solitary and lucid spectator of a multiform, instantaneous and almost intolerably precise world. Babylon, London and New York have overwhelmed with their ferocious splendor the imaginations of men; no one, in their populous towers or their urgent avenues, has felt the heat and pressure of a reality as indefatigable as that which day and night converged upon the hapless Ireneo, in his poor South American suburb. It was very difficult for him to sleep. To sleep is to turn one's mind from the world; Funes, lying on his back on his cot in the shadows, could imagine every crevice and every molding in the sharply defined houses surrounding him. (I repeat that the least important of his memories was more minute and more vivid than our perception of physical pleasure or physical torment.) Towards the east, along a stretch not yet divided into blocks, there were new houses, unknown to Funes. He imagined them to be black, compact, made of homogeneous darkness; in that direction he would turn his face in order to sleep. He would also imagine himself at the bottom of the river, rocked and annihilated by the current.

With no effort, he had learned English, French, Portuguese and Latin. I suspect, however, that he was not very capable of thought. To think is to forget differences, generalize, make abstractions. In the teeming world of Funes, there were only details, almost immediate in their presence.

The wary light of dawn entered the earthen patio.

Then I saw the face belonging to the voice that had spoken all night long. Ireneo was nineteen years old; he had been born in 1868; he seemed to me as monumental as bronze, more ancient than Egypt, older than the prophecies and the pyramids. I thought that each of my words (that each of my movements) would persist in his implacable memory; I was benumbed by the fear of multiplying useless gestures.

Ireneo Funes died in 1889, of congestion of the lungs.

The Authors

Ilse Aichinger

novelist, short-story writer, and poetess was born in 1921 in Vienna. She spent her childhood in Vienna and Linz and, after the war, studied medicine for several semesters. Her first novel, *Die grössere Hoffnung*, was published in 1948. She now resides in Upper Bavaria with her husband, German poet Günter Eich. In 1952 she received the prize of the "Group 47."

MAJOR WORKS: *Die grössere Hoffnung* (1948) tr. *Herod's Children* (1963), *Der Gefesselte* (1953) tr. *The Bound Man and Other Stories* (1956). Other collections of her poems and stories include *Zu keiner Stunde* (1957), *Wo ich wohne* (1963), *Eliza, Eliza; Erzählungen* (1965), and one translated miscellany: *Selected Short Stories and Dialogues* (1966).

Isaac Babel

playwright and short-story writer, was born in Odessa in 1894. He studied at the University of Saratov, and moved to St. Petersburg in 1915. Babel's first short stories, influenced by de Maupassant and Flaubert, were written in French. In 1916 he met Maxim Gorky, who arranged for the publication of two of his stories. During the Revolution, Babel served for a while with Budyonny's cavalry. His best-known collection of short stories about life in the cavalry appeared in 1926. Babel was arrested in 1939 and it is believed that he died in a concentration camp in 1941.

MAJOR WORKS: *Odessa Tales*, 1924; *Benya Krik*, 1926; *Red Cavalry*, 1926.
English Translations: *Collected Stories*, 1955; *Lyubka the Cossack and Other Stories*, 1963; *The Lonely Years*, 1964, a collection of unpublished short stories and letters from 1925–1939.

Albert Camus

novelist, playwright, and essayist, was born in Mondovi, Algeria in 1913. He graduated from the University of Algiers in 1936 with a degree in philosophy. For several years he directed an Algerian theater company. In 1942 he joined the French Resistance movement and became editor of the clandestine newspaper *Combat*. One year later he published *The Myth of Sisyphus,* one of his most important and influential philosophical works; the same year he accepted a position as editor at the Gallimard publishing house in Paris, a job he held until his death. Camus received the Nobel Prize in literature in 1957. His life ended prematurely in an automobile accident on January 4, 1960.

MAJOR WORKS: Camus's philosophical works include *Le Mythe de Sisyphe* (1943) tr. *The Myth of Sisyphus* (1955), and *L'Homme révolté* (1951) tr. *The Rebel* (1954). His four plays, *Caligula* (1944) tr. *Caligula, Le Malentendu* (1944) tr. *The Misunderstanding, L'Etat de Siège* (1948) tr. *State of Siege,* and *Les Justes* (1950) tr. *The Just Assassins* have appeared in one volume, *Caligula and Three Other Plays* (1958). His novels include *L'Etranger* (1942) tr. *The Stranger* (1946), *La Peste* (1947) tr. *The Plague* (1948), and *La Chute* (1956) tr. *The Fall* (1957). He also published a collection of short stories, *L'Exil et le Royaume* (1957) tr. *Exile and the Kingdom* (1957).

Gottfried Benn

poet, essayist, and short-story writer, was born in 1886 in the Mark Brandenburg, Germany. He was the son of a minister and first studied theology and literature, but soon changed to medicine. During World War I he served in the me⸱ ⸱cal corps of the German army. He was briefly attracted to the political theories of Nazism, but he soon rejected its cultural goals; consequently, his work was banned. He rejoined the army in 1935 and served in the medical corps during World War II. It was not until 1948, when he published a collection of poems in Switzerland, that Benn attained fame as a poet. In 1951 he received the Büchner Prize. Benn is still best known for his poetry, which had a tremendous influence on the post-war German poets. He died in West Berlin in 1956.

MAJOR WORKS: Collected works in 4 volumes, Limes Verlag, Wiesbaden, 1959–61. For a selection of his poetry and short stories translated into English see G. Benn: *Primal Vision,* ed. by E. B. Ashton.

Heinrich Böll

short-story writer and novelist was born in Cologne in 1917. Böll became known as a writer in 1951 when he received the Prize of the Group 47, an association of writers who started the new German literature after World War II. Böll's writing is directed against the uselessness of war and the emptiness of modern life. He finds his ancestors in writers like Charles Dickens, Wolfgang Borchert, Hemingway, and Faulkner. Böll started as a writer of short stories describing happenings in the lives of soldiers and ex-soldiers. In almost all his works he criticizes—in a manner similar to the moralistic outlook of Camus—society and its institutions. His latest novel *Views of a Clown* has stirred a great deal of contradiction and controversy. In this novel his social and political criticism has become even more relentless.

MAJOR WORKS: *Billard um halbzehn* (1959) tr. *Billiards at Half-past Nine* (1959), *Views of a Clown* (1963). For a collection of his short stories in English, see Böll: *18 Stories,* (1966).

Jorge Luis Borges

poet, essayist, and short-story writer was born in Buenos Aires in 1899. He traveled with his family to Europe and finished his secondary school education in Switzerland. After three years in Spain he returned to Buenos Aires in 1921. Until 1930 Borges wrote mainly poetry. He published his first book of poetry *El fervor de Buenos Aires* in 1923. After 1930 he turned to writing fiction and published *Ficciones,* his best known collection of stories, in 1944. In 1956 Borges received Argentina's National Prize of Literature, and in 1961 he shared with Samuel Beckett the International Publisher's Prize. Now almost entirely blind he spends most of his energy and time on teaching literature at the University of Buenos Aires. Borges has translated works by Gide, Faulkner, and Virginia Woolf. He was the first one to translate the works of Kafka into Spanish.

MAJOR WORKS: *Ficciones* (1945) tr. *Ficciones* (1962); *El Aleph* (1949), a collection of short stories; *Otras inquisiciones* (1952) tr. *Other Inquisitions* (1965), his most important collection of essays; *El hacedor* (1960) tr. *Dream-tigers* (1964). For other translations, see *Labyrinths* (1962), a collection of stories, essays, and parables.

Franz Kafka

novelist and short-story writer, was born in 1883 in Prague, the son of a well-to-do middle class Jewish merchant. He received his law degree at the German University of Prague in 1906. For many years he worked in an insurance company. In 1923 he moved from Prague to Berlin. However, only one year later he had several severe attacks of tuberculosis which forced him to go at the early age of forty-one to a sanatorium in Vienna where he died of this disease in June 1924. The publication of Kafka's works is due to the indefatigable efforts of his friend Max Brod. After Kafka's death Max Brod published, against Kafka's expressed will, the manuscripts which Kafka himself had not destroyed. Kafka's thinking is deeply rooted in Pascal and Kierkegaard.

MAJOR WORKS: *In der Strafkolonie* (1919) tr. *The Penal Colony, Stories and Short Pieces* (1948); *Der Prozess* (1925) tr. *The Trial* (1937); *Das Schloss* (1926) tr. *The Castle* (1930); *Amerika* (1927) tr. *America* (1938); *Beim Bau der chinesischen Mauer* (1931)) tr. *The Great Wall of China and Other Pieces* (1946); *Parabolen* (1935) tr. *Parables* (1947); *Hochzeitsvorbereitungen auf dem Lande und andere Prosa aus dem Nachlass* (1953) tr. *Dearest Father, Stories and Other Writings* (1954); *The Diaries of Franz Kafka* (tr. 1948–49).

Pär Lagerkvist

novelist, dramatist, and poet was born in Växjö, Sweden in 1891. While studying at the University of Upsala in 1911–12, Lagerkvist published his first work, a few poems and a naturalistic novella, *Människor*. However, the influence of the cubist movement in modern painting caused him to abandon the techniques of naturalism in favor of a style reminiscent of the parable or the fable. During the first two decades of the twentieth century, Lagerkvist devoted himself to the writing of plays and, for a brief period, was theater critic of a Stockholm newspaper. In 1940 he was elected to the Swedish Academy, and in 1951 he was awarded the Nobel Prize in literature.

MAJOR WORKS: Lagerkvist's novels in English translation include *The Dwarf* (1945), *Barabbas* (1951), *The Sibyl* (1958), *The Death of Ahasuerus* (1962), and *The Pilgrim at Sea* (1964). His latest work, *The Holy Land*, was published in 1966. Most of his major short works are included in a collected translation entitled *The Eternal Smile And Other Stories* (1954). Two of Lagerkvist's plays, *The Man Without A Soul* and *Let Man Live* have been included in *Scandinavian Plays of the Twentieth Century* (1944, 1951). A third, *Midsummer Dream in the Workhouse* (1953) has also been translated.

Alberto Moravia

novelist, short-story writer, and journalist was born in Rome in 1907, the son of a prosperous and cultivated architect. With the help of his governesses he learned French, English, and German. At the age of nine a severe tuberculosis of the leg bone made him an invalid for the next nine years the last two of which he spent in a sanatorium in the Alps. Early in his life he became acquainted with the works of Shakespeare and Molière, who had a great influence on his literary development. The publication of his first novel, *The Time of Indifference*, caused a sensation and made Moravia famous at the age of twenty-two. For several years he worked as a journalist for the Milan newspaper *Corriere della Sera*, a job which took him to Paris, London, Athens, and Mexico. Due to serious conflicts with the Fascist regime Moravia's works were banned and he started publishing articles under a pseudonym. During the German occupation of Italy he had to hide for nine months in the mountains and live with his wife in a pigsty until the Allied Forces liberated Italy.

MAJOR WORKS: *Gli indifferenti* (1929) tr. *The Time of Indifference* (1953); *Agostino* (1945) published together with *La disubbidienza* as *Two Adolescents*; *The Stories of Agostino and Luca* (1950); *La Romana* (1947) tr. *The Woman of Rome* (1949); *L'amore coniugale* (1949) tr. *Conjugal Love* (1951); *Il disprezzo* (1954) tr. *A Ghost at Noon* (1955); *La Ciociara* (1957) tr. *Two Women* (1958); *La noia* (1960) tr. *The Empty Canvas* (1961); for English translations of the stories, see *Bitter Honeymoon* (1956), *Roman Tales* (1957), *The Wayward Wife* (1960), *More Roman Tales* (1964), and *Fetish and Other Stories* (1965).

Cesare Pavese

poet, novelist, and short-story writer, was born in Cuneo, Italy, in 1908. He studied literature, especially American literature, at Turin University, and started a long series of translations from American and English writers. After Pavese had received his degree with a thesis on Walt Whitman, he taught for a while. Then he became editor of the review *La Cultura*. His articles written against the Fascist regime and published in this journal caused his arrest together with other members of the staff of *La Cultura* in May 1935. He was charged with anti-Fascist activities and had to serve ten months of preventive detention. Between 1936–1949 he wrote most of his novels and short stories. He committed suicide in August 1950 when he was not quite forty-two years old.

MAJOR WORKS: *Il diavolo sulle colline* (1949) tr. *The Devil in the Hills* (1959); *Tra donne sole* (1949) tr. *Among Women Only* (1959); *Dialoghi con Leucò* (1947) tr. *Dialogues with Leuco* (1964); *La luna e il falò* (1950) tr. *The Moon and the Bonfires* (1953); *Il mestiere di vivere* (1952) tr. *The Burning Brand: Diaries 1935–1950* (1961). *Notte di festa* (1953), a collection of his short stories written between 1936 and 1938, tr. *Festival Night and Other Stories* (1964).

Luigi Pirandello

playwright, novelist, and short-story writer, was born in Agrigento, Sicily, in 1867. He started his literary training in the schools of Palermo and Rome and received his doctorate at the University of Bonn in 1891. Pirandello's first literary attempts were poems, but he soon turned to writing fiction under the influence of his friend Capuana. Financial difficulties forced Pirandello to teach at a girl's school in Rome. The teaching and the insanity of his wife became a constant burden for him. By 1918 he was able to quit teaching and live on his royalities. Today Pirandello is best known for his plays. However, the writing of plays did not really start until 1916, after he had already published several novels and many short stories. Pirandello became a public figure between 1922 and 1924. Even Mussolini expressed admiration for his works, which enabled Pirandello to open his Art Theatre in 1925. His company traveled to Vienna, Prague, Budapest, Paris, London, to the leading cities in Germany, and also to Argentina and Brazil. In 1934 Pirandello was awarded the Nobel Prize. He died in 1936.

MAJOR WORKS: Pirandello wrote more than thirty plays, the best-known of which are: *Sei personaggi in cercae d'autore* (1921) tr. *Six Characters in Search of an Author* and *Enrico IV* (1922) tr. *Henry IV*, available together with other plays in *Naked Masks* (1952). His best-known novel is *Il Fu Mattia Pascal* (1904) tr. *The Late Mattia Pascal* (1964). His stories are collected in 15 volumes: *Novelle per un anno* (1932–37); for English translations, see Luigi Pirandello: *Short Stories* (1959), *Short Stories* (1965), and *The Merry-Go-Round of Love and Selected Stories* (1964).

Jean-Paul Sartre

philosopher, novelist, and playwright, was born in Paris in 1905. He took his degree in philosophy at the Ecole Normale Supérieure in 1929. In 1933–34 he studied philosophy in Germany under Edmund Husserl and Martin Heidegger. Through his literary essays he introduced Faulkner and Hemingway to the French public. During the Second World War he served in the French army and was taken prisoner by the Germans in 1940. He was released after nine months, whereupon he returned to Paris and joined the Résistance, writing for such underground publications as *Les Lettres Françaises* and Albert Camus's *Combat*. At that time his play *The Flies* had attracted wide attention in occupied

Paris. In 1946 Sartre founded the review *Les Temps Modernes,*
the journal which later served as the battleground for the ideological
dispute between Sartre and Camus. Awarded the Nobel Prize
in 1964, Sartre declined it, arguing that his philosophical and
political principles made it impossible for him to accept the award.

MAJOR WORKS: Sartre's philosophical works include *L'Imagination* (1936) tr. *Psychology and Imagination* (1948); *L'Etre et le
Néant* (1943) tr. *Being and Nothingness* (1956); and *L'Existen-
tialisme est un humanisme* (1946) tr. *Existentialism* (1947).
Novels and Short Stories: *La Nausée* (1938) tr. *Nausea* (1949);
Le Mur (1939) tr. *The Wall and Other Stories* (1948); the in-
complete novel cycle *Les Chemins de la Liberté* including *L'Age
de Raison* (1945) tr. *The Age of Reason* (1947), *Le Sursis* (1945)
tr. *The Reprieve* (1947), and *La Mort dans l'Ame* (1949) tr.
Troubled Sleep (1951); *Les Mots* (1964) tr. *The Words* (1964).
Plays: *Les Mouches* (1943) tr. *The Flies* (1947); *Huis Clos*
(1944) tr. *No Exit* (1947); *La Putain Respectueuse* (1946) tr.
The Respectful Prostitute (1949); *Les Mains Sales* (1948) tr.
Dirty Hands (1949); *Les Séquestrés d'Altone* (1960) tr. *The Condemned of Altona* (1961).

Afterword

While the short story as a genre has a long history, and although it receives a good deal of critical attention, there is still wide variation in the definitions offered to distinguish it from other forms of narrative fiction. Any serious attempt at a single definition, which would embrace the variety of existing representations of the story, is impossible. Therefore, it might be more helpful to define the short story not as an isolated phenomenon, but in relation to its most conspicuous counterpart—the novel.

Great novelists have seldom been prolific short-story writers, and good short-story writers have often failed in the creation of novels. Maupassant, one of the most important short-story writers at the end of the nineteenth century, never succeeded in producing a really good novel, although he covered a greater range and variety of experiences and situations than did Flaubert in his novels. Maupassant, like Chekhov, exhausted all the possible aspects of his characters' social, psychological, and intellectual surroundings, whereas Flaubert, like Dostoevsky, wrote variations of one monumental ideology. Balzac must have seen the need of presenting one huge novel, when he imposed the idea of the *Comédie Humaine* as one unifying theme in which each novel formed a small part of a greater unity which Balzac called the "Human Comedy."

The primary distinction between the novel and the short story is in the basic structure of the narrative. A novel is composed of a series of subactions of various sizes, each of which is unified but no one of which is fully independent since it contains elements tying it both to what has come before and what is to follow. A short story, on the other hand, takes an action of a certain size which serves as the unifying basis of the work; the action must be fully independent and self-contained. In the traditional novel, characters are exposed to a sequence of events. Under the immediate influence of these events, the outlooks and attitudes of the characters might undergo a slow change. The peculiar nature of the modern short story is similar to Rilke's image of the "Torso of an Archaic Apollo." A full and comprehensive view of the statue is unnecessary because the radiance of the torso suggests an intense unity. The torso, though only a part of the whole, radiates the power of the greater entity which is not described but suggested. The short story aspires to the intensity Rilke ascribed to the torso. The density and length of a short story thus depend on the different actions or non-actions it deals with. Generally, the action develops within one situation, and offers two possibilities to the character involved in the action. He can either change his way of viewing the world and his criteria for making value judgments, or he can remain static.

Novelists like Balzac, Flaubert, Stendhal, Dostoevsky, and later, Proust, Mann, and Joyce use their characters to portray ideologies. In Mann's *The Magic Mountain*, for example, there is the theme of Hans Castorp, the theme of Joachim Ziemssen, the theme of Behrens, and the theme of Settembrini. They are not merely characters; in their confrontations they are also the contrast, the clash, and the exchange of different ideological orientations. The tension springs from the dialectical progression of their ideological convictions. Each character exposes his own views, defends them, and establishes a constant polarity between himself and the other characters. He is involved in a process which enriches his own life. On the ideological level the novel competes to a certain extent with the moral and philosophical essay.

The variety of characters and their diverse ideologies, essential to the form of the novel, generally correspond to a long sequence of intense events and actions, which influence the characters' lives. The novelist reaches into the depths of the past, links past events to the present moment, and hopes to establish a continuity and recognizable order in the characters' development. The short-story writer has to impose greater restrictions on his art. He has neither the space nor the time to draw elaborate progressions from past to present happenings. The depiction of a series of facts and events gives way to the creation of a state of mind. The short-story writer has to move within the intricate web of a present situation; he generally ignores lines of chronological sequence, and limits himself to short glimpses of the past which might throw some light on the present. If the novelist is closely tied to the sequence of events, the short-story writer exhausts the density of a situation. The latter explores the uniqueness of an incident, and causes, as Edgar Allan Poe said, a certain unique or single effect. Therefore, it is not unusual that the short-story writer avoids the use of a traditional plot by reducing his story to an image. In Kafka's *Metamorphosis*, the metaphor is the story and the story is the metaphor. Freed from a consistent concern about aspects of an ideology, the short-story writer tries to evoke intense situations and emotions. With each story, he can become involved in an entirely new experience: there can be as many levels of reality as there are short stories. If the novelist strives for an ideological unity in the juxtaposition of his characters and actions, the short-story writer wants to focus on the intensity of a situation or an experience, and to create a mood which stimulates the creation of thoughts and ideas.

II

Jean-Paul Sartre, the French philosopher and writer, proclaimed in a precise phrase the new philosophical orientation and outlook of the twentieth century: "existence precedes essence." The brevity of this categorical statement is in no proportion to the explosive impact and influence of its meaning. His formulation breaks with the comfort and convenience of a long-established tradition in the western world, shakes its foundation, and reverses the dominant Kantian principle that essence precedes existence.

According to Sartre, and contrary to Kant, man's essence is not something given at the moment of his coming into existence; man has to create his essence at every single moment of his existence. Man is thrown into an abyss of nothingness; he struggles with his existence not to *search* for his essence, but to *create* it in his existence. Lacking all traditional values, man faces himself in his threatening loneliness. He can no longer rely on an accepted framework of values, since he himself becomes the maker of his own values. At the end of Sartre's play *No Exit* the characters are faced with the possibility of escaping their sadistic and torturous existence in hell by choosing to leave the prison through the open door. Afraid of the uncertainty of the world outside their prison, they stay in the room and continue their miserable and humiliating existence within its walls.

Since Sartre vigorously rejects the notion of an established system which guides man from the very beginning of his existence, man finds himself in an entirely new and isolating situation. In the abyss of his own being he faces numerous possibilities among which he must choose in order to begin the long and never-ending struggle to create his own essence. The necessity of making a choice creates man's fear of failure, and his world becomes uncertain and insecure.

In *Flowers of Evil* (1857) Charles Baudelaire had already celebrated the abyss. Newness springs from the multiple possibilities of disorder inherent in the abyss, and not from the stagnation of order: "To plunge to the bottom of the abyss . . . to the bottom of the unknown in order to find something *new*!" ("Le Voyage") Baudelaire saw the abyss as the positive, strong source of his inspiration.

The roots of twentieth century sensibility extend deeply into the philosophical and aesthetic concepts of two nineteenth-century philosophers: Søren Kierkegaard and Friedrich Nietzsche. For

Kierkegaard there are no preconstructed answers to the problems of human life. Every situation, every action is new, unprecedented, without a prior solution. Kierkegaard rediscovered the possibilities of the present moment and drew attention away from a traditionally accepted transcendence in order to intensify the power of the present moment. He also pointed out the hazards which spring from the new awareness of all the possibilities inherent in the immediate reality. Each moment constitutes an intersection with innumerable new directions. Facing this intricate web of possibilities, man has to choose. The state of uncertainty preceding the act of choice causes his anguish, his *Angst*, which at the same time opens the gate to a spontaneous and authentic existence. For his part, Nietzsche had Zarathustra return from the mountains to declare that God was dead, thus disturbing the calm and self-sufficient reliance on an established, irrefutable, philosophical, and religious transcendence. The confidence born of a strong belief in God had been undermined, and an age of inner insecurity spread its first waves of change.

Gide, Proust, Kafka, Camus, and Sartre were among the first writers to reflect this uncertain atmosphere in their philosophical and literary works. These writers saw themselves in clear contrast to the nineteenth-century novelists, Balzac, Stendhal, and Flaubert, who believed in the solidity of the world in which they lived. Their *Weltanschauung* made it possible for them to conceive and construct characters who move within a stable framework of tradition, who are judged by a fixed hierarchy of social or ethical values. Balzac, especially, was eager to register and depict the minutest details of his surroundings. Scientific reproduction of the world in which he lived became a major artistic goal. The culmination of this attitude is evident in the novels of Emile Zola, who had worked out a scientific theory for the creation and interpretation of a novel.

When Kierkegaard and Nietzsche violently attacked the Christian tradition, they undermined concepts from which man had drawn nourishment for centuries, and helped to breed insecurity in the minds of the writers at the turn of the century. The objective, at times almost scientific, approach of the later nineteenth-century writers had to be abandoned, but a deep void followed the destruction. At the beginning of the twentieth century, many writers explored the depth of this void, and its persistent atmosphere haunts their works in heavy rhythms. Identity of character turns into non-identity, human characteristics exist through their absence, and the meaning of life disappears. Robert Musil entitled his novel *Man Without Qualities*.

Objectivity was supplanted by a more subjective outlook on the world. Proust's narrator in *Remembrance of Things Past* tries to recuperate and formulate all possible gradations of his past emotional and intellectual life. Concrete objects are dissolved and replaced by shades of interactivity between the object and the subject. The basic distrust of reality grows into a disbelief in accepted language. The third-person narrative, predominant in nineteenth-century writing, shifts to the "I" narrative. There is no longer just one reality and one language, but as many realities and languages as there are writers. The collapse of a generally accepted objective world order forced the writer to withdraw into himself and rely on his own subjective view of the world.

The lack of confidence in a common and universal reality and language opened up an explosive variety of subjective stylistic and aesthetic values. Whereas the nineteenth-century writer tended to favor a highly descriptive style, the modern writer creates a more dynamic one. Because life is presently seen as a never ending flux rather than a sequence of events, the movement of an action, not its consequence, is important. One of the forerunners of such fictional techniques was Henry James, who had sensed the unimportance of describing the result of an action. James habitually builds great lines of crescendoes in his actions, but generally omits the peak of such a development. Instead, he takes up the action after the event to follow new dynamic lines.

The modern writer shows a propensity to suggest rather than to state. Stylistically, the intensity of suggestion is increased when he uses the fragment. Furthermore, fragmentary presentation of emotions, thoughts, and sentences, in other words an incomplete reflection or transformation of an experience, forces the reader to participate in the literary work. He can no longer maintain the role of spectator; he becomes an actor deeply involved in the work of art. The act of reading becomes an act of creation.

The objective presentation of external reality no longer attracts the writer. He wants to go beyond the world of appearance and evoke the emotional and intellectual complexity and immediacy of man. If the writer rejects the depiction of external reality, he overcomes it by distorting it. Through distortion he hopes to reach the inner reality behind the external reality. He no longer adheres to the traditional concept of beauty, since he sees greater artistic possibilities in the ugly or in the juxtaposition of the beautiful and the ugly. Baudelaire had already been fascinated by the idea of the ugly and established for himself an aesthetic of ugliness. The fusion of the ugly and beautiful created a new level of mysterious beauty. An object which generally had been considered beautiful was too restricted and lacked the intensity of two incongruous objects brought together in an unusual juxtaposition. Stylistically, this juxtaposition often materializes in the metaphor—hence the frequent use of metaphor in modern fiction.

A metaphor combines disparate elements of two objects, and suggests an atmosphere rather than describing it. It is through the metaphor that the writer quite often conveys his most personal view of the world.

The absence of a comforting orientation either in the past or in the present also leads to a questioning of present reality. What seems to be reality might only be an illusion of reality. Luigi Pirandello made this strange dichotomy the subject of his play *Six Characters in Search of an Author*, in which a continuous, at times confusing, interaction of the real and the fictitious takes place. Six real characters enter from the outside to have their personal tragedy performed in the environment of a fictitious world, the stage. The constant polarity between the real characters and the stage actors effaces the borderline between reality and illusion. The final shock of utter confusion comes at the end of the play when the death of the boy is not an act on the stage, an action portrayed by an actor, but a true tragedy: the boy kills himself.

Benn and Borges place some of the characters in their short stories in the state between reality and dream, where the dream world becomes reality, or reality dream. The main character of Borges's story *The Circular Ruins* wants to dream a man. When he succeeds, he is suddenly struck by the strange and disturbing thought that perhaps he himself is merely the dream of another man. Reality and illusion have ceased to be two distinctly separated realms. One can replace the other, and at times illusion seems to be more real than external reality. Man constantly sways between the two states of illusion and reality, and loses all sense of a comforting orientation. Each level of awareness and belief is immediately threatened by the possibility of a new recognition which questions the validity of the former level.

These aesthetic trends in modern literature make it clear that a new conception of the interaction between subject and object has evolved. Man as portrayed in modern fiction is characterized by a fundamental distrust and disbelief in an objective reality, which estranges him from his immediate surroundings. Physical closeness to external reality cannot overshadow the fact that spiritually he lives on a lonely island, completely separated from the objects around him. His physical proximity to familiar objects only makes him more aware of his psychic distance from them. Consequently, his effort of self-realization freezes in the contact with the outside world. The awareness of the disparity between the will to become authentic and the impossibility of its realization creates the feeling of the absurd. Camus, Sartre, Böll, Benn, to name only a few, explore the absurd states that afflict modern man. Meursault, the main character of Camus's *The Stranger*, slowly awakens to the absurdity of his own life, rejects the empty forms of his environment, rebels against tradition, and is punished for his attempt to be authentic in his feeling and thinking. The absurdity and monotony of modern man's situation is best illustrated in Camus's reinterpretation of the myth of Sisyphus. Sisyphus has been condemned by the gods to roll a rock to the top of a mountain. Once he reaches the top, the rock rolls down and Sisyphus has to start all over again.

Man then remains in a vast, indifferent monotony, unless he chooses to face, through an act of lucid introspection, the divorce between himself and the world in which he lives. The moment he sees and accepts the absurd confrontation of his own self with a meaningless world, he has taken the first step toward the realization of his authenticity. The first step will be followed by many others, but never by the last one, because a stagnant state of authentic existence is its very negation. Sisyphus, the miserable victim of the rock at first, becomes superior to his punishment when he steps outside his own predicament and lucidly views his own absurdity. The levels of absurdity vary with the levels of awareness. To assume that absurdity could be defined in abstract terms would be another absurdity. If it is true that life springs from some kind of polarity, then the notion of the absurd is one form of polarity. The disparity man discovers between himself and the world creates a continuous polarity, which keeps him alive. The *Angst* that threatens to overwhelm him in this gap cannot be accidental; it is a necessary stimulus to reach higher levels of awareness. Especially writers like Pavese, Pirandello, Moravia, Camus, Sartre, and Böll explore and reflect the anguish and distress man experiences when he sees himself swaying between the world and his authentic being. None of these writers, however, reaches the point where the characters in their stories have broken through to an authentic existence. The characters are portrayed in a state of becoming, and not in a state of arrival.

Disharmony increases suggestion far beyond the range and possibility of harmony. The short-story writer relies on the power inherent in images and metaphors. Through the clash of disparate elements in a metaphor or in an image, he suggests more than he could ever abstractly say. The disharmonic tension creates an intense atmosphere conducive to the formulation of thoughts and ideas. It is the great advantage of disharmony that it always goes beyond itself and opens new realms of suggestion. In these moments, the short story reaches the intensity and suggestiveness of an intellectually guided poetry.